C000002816

These stories are deep exister
us lack not only a place but
Listening to their lament w
hopefully move us toward
blessings in which our hospitality, skills and companionship
will reconfigure both of our worlds.
Marijke Hoek, author, theologian and regular media contributor

Dave Smith is one of those inspirational people who make a
real and lasting difference to the lives of those who meet
them. He is not afraid to take up the causes of those who are
most marginalised, yet he is never bowed down by the many
desperate stories he hears. You don't have to share his deep
Christian faith to admire his work, but it is that faith which is
his strength and his motivation. In this book he invites us,
with his customary warmth and compassion, to go with him
to the world of just a small sample of those he has met as
founder of the Boaz Trust. It's a journey well worth taking.
Bishop David Walker, Bishop of Manchester

Dave Smith's book is both challenging and insightful and is
essential reading if you want to get a deeper understanding
of how refugees make the decision to leave their homes and
families and how they cope when their applications for
protection in the UK are rejected and they are left destitute.
Perhaps its greatest achievement is allowing the reader to see
the seven protagonists as ordinary people who are struggling
to rebuild their lives in the most difficult of circumstances,
rather than as statistics, victims, or the subjects of tabloid
headlines.
Mike Kaye, Advocacy Manager, Still Human Still Here coalition

There is no better way to understand the world of refugees than to hear their stories in their own words. This book is gripping reading. I thoroughly recommend it.

Martin Charlesworth, Team Leader, Jubilee Plus and Elder at Barnabas Community Church, Shrewsbury

Storytelling is empowering, releasing; it builds bridges, makes connections and brings healing for the teller and the listener. It has been hijacked by soulless decision making processes within the asylum system and we need to recapture its magic. Dave Smith has the track record, the respect, the dedication and the storytelling gift to bring these stories together, and to present these extraordinary and courageous lives in detail, which demands attention. I commend this work very highly; be ready to be stretched and to feel you have to do something.

Tiffy Allen, National Coordinator, City of Sanctuary

REFUGEE STORIES

Seven personal journeys
behind the headlines

DAVE SMITH

instant
apostle

First published in Great Britain in 2016

Instant Apostle
The Barn
1 Watford House Lane
Watford
Herts
WD17 1BJ

British Library Cataloguing-in-Publication Data

A catalogue record for this book is available from the British Library.

This book and all other Instant Apostle books are available from Instant Apostle:
Website: www.instantapostle.com
E-mail: info@instantapostle.com

ISBN 978-1-909728-48-6

Printed in Great Britain

Instant Apostle is a way of getting ideas flowing, between followers of Jesus, and between those who would like to know more about His Kingdom.

It's not just about books and it's not about a one-way information flow. It's about building a community where ideas are exchanged. Ideas will be expressed at an appropriate length. Some will take the form of books. But in many cases ideas can be expressed more briefly than in a book. Short books, or pamphlets, will be an important part of what we provide. As with pamphlets of old, these are likely to be opinionated, and produced quickly so that the community can discuss them.

Well-known authors are welcome, but we also welcome new writers. We are looking for prophetic voices, authentic and original ideas, produced at any length; quick and relevant, insightful and opinionated. And as the name implies, these will be released very quickly, either as Kindle books or printed texts or both.

Join the community. Get reading, get writing and get discussing!

Dedication

I would like to dedicate this book to Alpha Bah, one of the first destitute asylum seekers that we housed at the Boaz Trust. He taught me, in three words, pretty much everything you need to know about life for an asylum seeker in the UK. Many times he would sigh, and say, 'You know Dave, *it's not easy.*'

The British are famous for their use of the understatement; Guineans, like Alpha, are not – yet that phrase has stuck in my head for the past ten years since I first heard him say it. Contrary to what you may have read in some newspapers, life is anything but easy for the asylum seeker in the UK.

And I also hope that you may be moved, as I and many others have been, when faced with the reality of those seeking sanctuary in our green and pleasant land, not just to agree with us, but please – do something about it.

Contents

Foreword..13

Introduction..15

Hanes' story...22

Ayesha's story 47

Maron's story 68

Mary's story...100

Sheikh's story 130

Kundai's story..156

Rep's story 188

The current refugee crisis 231

About Dave Smith 246

Foreword

It is easy to be daunted by the enormous scale of refugee displacement in the Middle East and North Africa today, let alone in the rest of the world. Though the UK only provides protection to a very small proportion of the tiny minority who make it to Europe in search of safety, looking at much of our media you'd be forgiven for thinking that the UK was in the grip of an existential refugee crisis.

How we overcome the relentless negativity of this dominant public narrative is the terrain this book explores, though not by the deployment of rhetoric or polemics or statistics, but simply by enabling people who've sought refugee in the UK from violence, bigotry, oppression and persecution in their countries of origin, to tell their stories, in their way, using their words.

These stories enable us to look at the world through the eyes of those who have been forced to flee their homes, their families and their friends; those who have experienced the terror of persecution and the desolation of exile; those who have made punishing and brutal journeys and who live with the constant echo of loss and pain.

In a world where the stereotyping of asylum seekers and refugees and the pitting of the deserving refugee against the undeserving migrant have become commonplace in public and political discourse, the resonantly and defiantly human stories in this compelling book provide the strongest antidote to the poison of scapegoating, by triggering our empathy, that most empowering of human characteristics.

Maurice Wren, Chief Executive, Refugee Council

Introduction

When I wrote *The Book of Boaz*,[1] I desperately wanted to show that life in the UK for those seeking asylum here is vastly different from the misinformation peddled by the tabloid media. The only way to do that was to include short stories of some of those I had come to know in the 15 years since I first met an asylum seeker.

It is never easy to find asylum seekers who are willing to tell their stories. There are good reasons for this. For some the memories of death and destruction from which they fled are still so raw that they cannot face reliving them. Others fear that, by revealing in the media what happened to them, their enemies will be able to identify them and find them, which could endanger their own lives even here in the UK, and would almost certainly endanger the lives of their loved ones back home.

Those who are still in the process of seeking asylum inevitably fear that anything they say may prejudice their ongoing case, so they are the least likely to want to talk. And even when they are accepted as refugees, most will just want to forget the past and simply get on with their new life here. They just want to be *normal*, with a home, a job, a family, doing the ordinary things that we take for granted and which, to be honest, sometimes bore us.

For the last ten years or so I have tried hard to respond to journalists' requests for interviews with asylum seekers, but I have rarely been able to oblige. Sometimes journalistic deadlines are totally unrealistic. So are their requirements: 'Female victim of rape from the Congo aged under 30 living in Manchester, willing to do a TV interview by tomorrow…' I don't think so! Or, more recently, in the wake of the harrowing pictures from the so-called 'refugee crisis',[2] numerous requests for a 'Syrian family that has just arrived in the UK and is living with a family', ignoring the fact that a) the UK had not taken any Syrians at that time and b) they were not going to be placed in families anyway!

Locating the right person, briefing them and ensuring that what is reported is both accurate and fair are not five-minute jobs, and the well-being of the asylum seeker has to be the priority. Even honourable, sympathetic and well-meaning journalists are often disappointed. One young reporter said he wanted to follow the life of an asylum seeker from the day they came into the UK. That's a great idea, but how could that happen? The Home Office would never cooperate. The only way would be to physically go and find an asylum seeker in the queues at Heathrow or Gatwick. I can't imagine he would have much success at Arrivals, carrying a board saying 'Asylum Seeker wanted for BBC interview'. That's why this book of stories is needed.

Storytelling as therapy

I don't profess to know much about psychology, but I do know this – there is something very therapeutic in being able to tell your story. For those whose asylum claims were turned down, who felt that those in authority never really listened to them, did not believe them, did not give them the opportunity to tell it in their own way and time – this is their opportunity to be listened to.

For those who have heard bits here and there about why people come and what happens to them in the UK asylum system, and want to know more – this is your opportunity to go deeper.

And for me, who really wanted to get under the skin of those I have met, and understand what they were thinking, feeling and doing through the whole process of escape, flight, arrival and ultimate safety – this was my opportunity too.

Who was included, and why?

I have chosen seven stories – four men, three women – so that there is plenty of variety, yet enough time and space to honour the storyteller. There is variety in the countries that the people come from – their ages, their backgrounds, their religions and education, their gender, their grounds for claiming asylum, and above all their personalities.

All seven have had something to do with the Boaz Trust or Mustard Tree charity, from which Boaz emerged. Most were accommodated in Boaz houses or with host families for a while. I had already met them all, and chose them to reflect that variety. Some I know very well, others not so well, but wanted to find out more.

Although they are all unique, they have these things in common:

- All were refused asylum in the UK and were made destitute.

- All except one have gone on to eventually get refugee status or discretionary leave to remain in the UK.

- All are people with skills to offer the UK, and are now giving back far more than they ever received in benefits or other forms of assistance.

I have included the one who is still living in limbo after many years so that you will understand that not every story has a happy ending. Refugee stories are definitely not fairy tales.

Many of those featured have had encounters with God during their life journey. I didn't choose them for that reason, although I got to know some of them better because of that encounter. I definitely have *not* coerced them into saying anything about Christianity or the Boaz Trust that they did not offer voluntarily. It's their story, not mine, and they have told it in their own way.

Why no Syrians?

There are no Syrians, not because I didn't want to include them, but thus far I have not met any, except for one man who spent some time in our night shelter, whom I cannot claim to know.

We all know, or think we know, what is going on in Syria. We have seen the bombing, the chaos, the destruction and the exodus across the Mediterranean, the dead bodies of young and old, and the procession across Europe heading for safety. I have no doubt that there are dozens of writers working on books about Syria right now, and hopefully including some real refugee stories in them. You don't need me to write another one.

I am appalled by the plight of the Syrians, and have signed the petitions calling for our government to take far more than the paltry 20,000 they have pledged to take over five years. Towards the end of the book I have written more about the refugee crisis, and how, even within the crisis, facts and figures are being deliberately distorted by senior politicians for political ends.

The bottom line is this: if we portray the refugee crisis to be just about Syria, or pretend that Syrians are genuine refugees and the rest fleeing with them are just 'economic migrants', then we have failed to understand both what a refugee is, and that the problem is worldwide, not just confined to a bit of the Middle East.

By focusing on Syria alone, it would be very easy to push even further into the background the tens of thousands of genuine refugees who are being refused asylum in the UK every year and deliberately subjected to a life of destitution. *Theirs* are the voices that have to be heard.

How were the stories collected?

I obtained their stories in a series of recorded, informal interviews – more like chats over a cup of coffee, really – and put them into writing. They are not transcribed verbatim: I have tried to preserve the authenticity of the teller's own voice, while also maintaining clarity for the reader.

I have kept the stories in the first person, but edited out, for the most part, bad grammar and incorrect use of English. I have left in the words and turns of phrase that they like to use, so that their personality shines through. In some cases, because of their limited English, the sentences are short and simple, but hopefully none the less powerful for that. I resisted the temptation to use an interpreter because, although it might lead to a more eloquent story, it often inhibits the narrator.

In every case the storyteller has read and approved the final version. I hope that the result is readable, challenging, educational and moving. Hearing the stories first-hand was certainly a very moving and emotional experience for me.

In some cases names have been changed, either to protect the storyteller or the other person. In those cases there is an asterisk (*) next to the name. Mary has changed her name to reflect her new Christian faith rather than any other reason. In one story you will find virtually no names at all, because of the sensitivity of the ongoing situation.

All proceeds from the book will go to the Boaz Trust. Of course, I would like it to sell in millions, but above all my dream is that it will change hearts and minds, so that future generations of asylum seekers are understood, treated with dignity and welcomed into the UK.

I won't say 'Enjoy the book'. It's not really a book for enjoying, but I do hope that you will celebrate with me those featured who represent, in their diversity and in their common humanity, the tens of thousands of refugees flooding north through Europe.

If there is one question that I would like you to take away at the end of this book, it would be this: 'How can a civilised country like the UK have refused asylum to those refugees, leaving them in destitution and despair?' And perhaps you may be moved enough to do more than just ask the question: I would love you to be part of the answer.

---

[1] Published by Instant Apostle, 2014.

[2] It apparently only became a 'crisis' when it came to Europe! It has been a crisis for Africa and the Middle East for decades, with millions of refugees in overflowing camps in Pakistan, Iran, Turkey, Kenya, Lebanon, Jordan and many more countries near the centres of conflict. Often it is referred to as a *migrant* crisis. Perhaps this is because acknowledging people as *refugees* assumes a moral obligation to help them.

Hanes' story

I was born and grew up in Bale Robe in Oromia state, in southern Ethiopia. Robe is the capital city of the Bale province, with a population of around 100,000.[3]

Ethiopia has two different histories. If you listen to my side of the story, maybe you will get confused. If you listen to someone that comes from the North, they have a different identity, a different religion, a different political opinion. They will tell you something different from me. I come from the South. We are an oppressed people. The Oromo people make up nearly 50 per cent of the population. For 100 years we had lost our identity. Even 25 years ago we could be put in prison for speaking our own language in our own land. That was the reality for the Oromo.[4] Things have changed, but there is still discrimination today. Hundreds of people still get arrested and beaten up for wanting self-rule.

I am not proud to be Ethiopian. In the UK, if you are British, you have rights. You also have obligations. If you are a citizen, you have to have rights. I have never felt Ethiopian, because nothing in my identity marks me out as Ethiopian. If I go to Addis Ababa, the land belongs to me, but I can't see anything I can identify with from my language, my culture, my religion or political opinion there. Ethiopia for me is not my home – it's like a second home. They force me to be Ethiopian. We can be Ethiopian through negotiation, like Scotland in the UK, but you can't force us to feel Ethiopian. We don't want independence – we just want self-determination, and the right to be treated as equals with everyone else in Ethiopia.

Yet you can't have Ethiopia without Oromia, because there are people from all the different tribes living among the Oromo people. If you go to the Amhara or Tigre regions, you will only see people from there: in Tigre they only speak Tigrinya. You won't find any Oromo there. Yet in Oromia they force their language and religion on you. That's discrimination. It's also true that Ethiopia needs Oromia: it's a rich and fertile region. It's the backbone of Ethiopia.

My childhood was quite a happy one. My family were Muslim. Like many Ethiopian families we struggled to improve our situation. My parents came from a village. The reason they came to the city was to give us a better life from the beginning. So they sent me to an Islamic school as well as a normal state school. My father was a teacher of Islam: he dedicated his whole life to Islam. My mother worked too, selling coffee in the market, so we could have a good life. She always said that the most important thing was to give us a good education. I had one brother, who was younger than me, and seven sisters. I was in the middle.

I enjoyed school, laughing and playing with friends. I was always the top student in my class of about 50. I represented my school in many academic competitions, and my parents would buy me new things as a reward. But I remember clearly one occasion when I was seven: the teacher asked me to bring a poem in Amharic,[5] but my family didn't speak the Amharic language, and I struggled to do that – it was difficult for me to read in Amharic. I told him I couldn't do it, and he made me bend down; then he put my head between his legs, and he beat me on the back.

So I did well at school until I got to eighth grade in 1991 – I was about 15 years old. Then the Derg government[6] was overthrown by Tigreans, and everything changed. Many of the former opposition parties came together, including the OLF.[7] There was a big conference in London, and they all agreed to form a transitional government for two years. At that time many from the OLF came into our region, and began to educate us about our past. We began to hear and understand where we had come from – that we were Oromo. We became aware that we had been colonised 100 years earlier by the Northern tribes.

From that time on I became involved in politics. I read the newspapers and listened to the radio, and I spent all of my time learning about our Oromo history. I found out why we were so backward, why we weren't allowed to speak our own language in public. I learned that the Oromo language had been banned in 1890 by Menelek.[8] In the courts you had to get everything translated into Amharic – even if the judge was Oromo. And in the Orthodox Church everything was in Amharic, and you couldn't be a priest if you were born in an Oromo family: they said that you weren't good enough to speak Amharic properly. They even taught that you wouldn't go to heaven if you spoke Oromo. Things have changed now: you can even learn Oromo in school, but there is still discrimination.

I don't have any problem with people from other tribes. There are good people in the Amhara and Tigre tribes, but the problem is the elite.[9]

At that time the OLF, even though it was quite weak, managed to get a lot of changes passed. The country adopted a federal system, and Oromia was one of the nine new states. Oromo was taught in school, and was allowed to be used in public buildings in the region. However, the OLF pulled out of the agreement after just one year and became a rebel organisation again, because it was being dominated by the Tigrean elite, who had all the military power.

As a result of spending so much time on my new interest in politics, my school grades dropped. I wanted to join the OLF, but I was too young at that time. But one of my sisters, who is three years older than me, left school and joined the military wing of the OLF.

When I became 18 in 1999, I also joined the OLF, and became very active. There were two parts to the OLF – the military wing and the civilian wing. I worked in the city, helping to set up and run cells. I helped to mobilise and organise the people in the cells. Each cell had five people in it, and none of the cells knew anyone from another cell. That way it was less dangerous: if someone was arrested and tortured, he couldn't tell the authorities anything about the other cells.

My job was also to collect money from relatives or business people to support the cells, as they did not have any income to carry out their work. Almost all those who were Oromo supported the OLF, including the intellectuals and the rich. Even many of the Oromo working in government were secretly supporting the OLF. On the surface they were part of the government, but if you scratched the surface, they were Oromo, and the OLF were working for their people.

My father had never been political. He didn't get involved at all. He wasn't even in business – he was a teacher of religion, but our family was under suspicion because my sister was fighting for the OLF. They didn't know about my activity at that time, but they were watching us. Then they started to put pressure on my father, as a leader in the mosque, to start encouraging his congregation to support the government. Many of the other imams had begun to support the OLF, and the government was trying to stop that. My father refused, not because he supported the OLF, but because he did not want to be involved politically. My parents didn't even know that my sister was going to run away to join the freedom fighters in the bush.

One night they came and took my father away. They had their heads covered, so we couldn't recognise them. The next day we found out he had been murdered. They had taken his body to the hospital and left it there. If people die in the police station, it's obvious who did it, but if they die in hospital, they can pretend that someone else did it, or say they don't know how it happened.

I was really upset, like all the family were. I had never expected it to happen like this. I could have understood it if he had been involved in politics; in that case you have to be prepared to pay the price, but he was never involved. It was the government's way of showing how strong they were, just demonstrating their brutality like this. Many people died in this way, even though they were not involved. They wanted to make the people scared, but it just made me more determined to take revenge on the regime. It made me stronger, and gave me more motivation.

My whole family was affected. Four of my sisters fled to other towns to stay with extended family, and I was left to support the rest of the family, so I had to get a job. I started to work with my mother, who had become tired, buying and selling coffee every Thursday in the market. At the same time I increased my work for the OLF. We never met in our house, because it was being watched. Instead we met at night in another OLF worker's house. It was dangerous, but there was no other option.

Then one of the men in our cell was arrested. When they tortured him, he mentioned my name. Three men came for me that night. They didn't show their ID, and they didn't have an arrest warrant. My mother tried to stop them, and fought with one of them, but he hit her over the head with his gun. Then they took me to a local prison, where they tortured me all night. They tied a rope around my neck that had metal inside. They didn't hang me. Instead they pushed me around, and beat me all over my body.

At the end of the night they took me to the hospital and left me for dead, just like my father – but I didn't die, thanks to Allah. I was young, and I recovered. The doctors operated on me, and I was in that hospital for 25 days. I still have the scars round my neck. After that, my family sent me to my uncle in Addis Ababa: they were afraid that the authorities would find out that I was not dead, and would come for me again. I stayed with my uncle Omar, who was a teacher, but went to the Kaliti hospital during the day for treatment and medicine.

Then the government discovered that I was still alive, and started looking for me. My mother had to flee, because they had started putting pressure on her again. I had been with my uncle for five months, and in May 2002 I began my journey to leave Ethiopia.

I had to change my ID card; I used my photo, but changed my name. It cost 50 Birr (about six dollars at the time). Then I caught the bus out of Addis with a friend of mine called Ziyad. His father was a very rich man, and he paid for everything. The bus took us to Shashamene, about 150 miles south of Addis. From there we were taken in the back of a lorry as far as Moyale on the Kenyan border. We knew that the authorities would be on the lookout for us, so we had to stay out of sight.

Moyale is a small town. It would have been difficult to cross if we had had our belongings with us – in that case we would have had to report at the border and have our documents stamped, but we didn't have proper passports, so we couldn't do that. There are two parts of Moyale: one part is in Ethiopia, and the other in Kenya. Lots of people work on the other side of the border, and you can just walk across if you don't take anything with you, so that's what we did. We crossed with the people going to work. The only thing we took was the money that Ziyad's father had given us, which we hid in our clothes.

Our aim was to get as far away as possible. First we had to cross Kenya to Nairobi. There were no buses, because the roads are very bad until you get to Nairobi. We found a lorry exporting cows to Kenya, and paid the driver to take us. We slept one night in Marsabit, about 200 miles from Nairobi. The second day the driver dropped us off, and we walked for about a day and a half until we were in Nairobi. But we knew that it was not safe, because the Ethiopian intelligence services were operating there,[10] and several OLF members had been abducted back to Ethiopia. One well-known OLF activist called Jatani Ali[11] had also been killed in Nairobi. So at that point we decided to head for South Africa. By now there were three of us. Another Ethiopian from the Hamara region (like Ziyad) had joined us in Kenya. Ziyad's father had also sent another US$2,000 when we were in Nairobi, so we thought we had enough money for the journey.

From Nairobi we crossed into Tanzania, not far from Mount Kilimanjaro. We could see it from the road. But it was difficult crossing the border, because we didn't have a passport. We found someone to help us cross illegally. There are a lot of police and military, but the border is big, so you can get across at night, but it's dangerous; we knew that some Ethiopians and Somalians had been eaten by lions, and others by crocodiles. It's not like the animals in the park in England!

We crossed the border with some Somalians, because they never have any papers. Everyone knows their country is broken: there is no central government, so they can travel across Africa without a passport. They thought we were Somalian, so we got through ok. When people get caught by the police, they say they are Somalian too.

Eventually we got to Dar es Salaam. Then we crossed into Malawi, but the people there were very poor, and we had nothing to eat. We even saw people selling roast rats on the streets, which was very strange for our culture. We bought mangoes to eat. Then we crossed into Mozambique.

By the time we got to Beira in Mozambique, we only had 50 dollars left between three Ethiopians. Beira is a very beautiful city by the Indian Ocean, with lots of Asians living there. We couldn't claim asylum in Mozambique: it is a very poor country, and it was difficult living there, even for their own people, but we didn't have enough money to get to South Africa. We talked about what we could do, and we decided to go and ask for help at the mosque and the churches. I went to the mosque, and they gave me about 30,000 in their money,[12] and the other two got about 200,000 from the church. That money helped us to catch a bus to Maputo on the Swaziland border. It was a full day's drive.

We spent one day in Maputo, then crossed the border into Swaziland illegally at night. That same night we crossed into South Africa. It had taken us 15 days to get there, but when we got into the country we were caught by a guy from the military at around midnight. He was smoking something – some sort of illegal drug. He kept us for six hours, and kept asking us for money. When he was high, he was saying he was going to put us in prison. Then when he came down, he would say that we could go, but all the time he was asking for money. We hadn't got any. I told him he could take my small radio, and one of my friends told him to take what he wanted from our bags. In the end, he took a few things from our bags. He gave us some directions and let us go at about six o'clock in the morning.

We had been walking for about ten minutes when a lady from the village called us over. She didn't speak English but communicated with her hands. She gave us some food made from maize – I think they call it mapp or something like that: in most of Africa they call it *ugali*.[13] We were really hungry. Then she directed us where to go. She made signs to tell us not to go a certain way, because that's where the police were.

When we got to the main road we started to beg for a lift. In Africa you do that by waving your hand. A lot of cars passed, but then this white guy came in a very nice car. He was driving fast because it was a big motorway. He stopped and started reversing towards us. At first we thought he was police or security, but he was just an ordinary guy. He asked us where we were going, and we said Johannesburg. He drove us all the way there. It took seven hours.

The journey had been really difficult. I was bitten by a mosquito on the way, and I got malaria. I didn't know where I was, who I was, or who took me to the hospital. I remember being in the car going there, but after that I don't remember anything. I was in hospital for five days, and at night I would wake up and not know if I was dead or alive. I had lost my mind. When I woke up I saw my hand and the glucose and medication going in. That's what I remember.

Crossing many borders in 15 days is so difficult. You're not driving there, or on a bus, or enjoying the journey. It's just your life. Sometimes it works, but many people die on the way. I left to escape prison, to seek sanctuary, but I was scared that I would be put in prison again. I didn't find sanctuary in Africa. When we got to South Africa we discovered that it was not a welcoming place. The ANC[14] were controlling the country, and there was a lot of mistrust of foreigners.[15]

We were in South Africa for a month. During that time we met many Oromo who told us how difficult life was in South Africa. They told us to go to the UK if we could. It was even dangerous in Johannesburg: there were a lot of asylum seekers in an area called Hillbrow, where there is a lot of crime. Often fights would break out there, and it wasn't safe.

When I was a little boy we learned about England. We learned that it was a beautiful country, how they helped to defeat the Nazis, how they took many refugees from Jewish communities – those are the kinds of things that we remember, that the teacher told us. We knew England had a reputation as a sanctuary for asylum seekers and was far away from trouble – that's why we had it in our mind to go to England and find sanctuary. That was my dream.

We were in Johannesburg for a week. Because we had no money left we slept in a big night shelter at night, and tried to find food in the day. There was no registration – anyone could stay there. There were hundreds of people in the shelter: lots of other Africans from many countries seeking asylum, and others too – some were drug addicts or drinkers. You had to take your bags with you during the day, because there was nowhere safe to leave them.

Hanes' journey through Africa

To the UK...

To get out of South Africa we needed passports, so Ziyad's father sent him 5,000 dollars. We couldn't get it before, because we didn't know anyone we could trust that he could send the money to. After about a week we found someone, an Oromo taxi driver who had been living there for a long time. He arranged to have the money sent to his bank, as we didn't have any way of accessing a bank. He also contacted an agent, who agreed to get all three of us out of the country for the whole 5,000 dollars.[16] I was going to London, and Ziyad to Germany. It depends on how desperate people are, and how much they have, as to what an agent will charge. For some people it may be as much as US$10,000.

The agent brought me on to the plane, and he kept my false passport the whole time. I never saw it: I didn't even know what the name was on it, whether it was my name or a different one. He never told me his name, or what he did, but I think he must have been a businessman who travelled all over Europe.[17] On the flight I never felt comfortable, wondering what was going to happen. The flight was 12 hours. The agents always use direct flights, because you might get caught in transit during a stopover. The stewardesses came round with breakfast in the morning, but I just couldn't eat anything. I was too nervous.

We arrived at Heathrow around nine or ten o'clock on 4th August 2002. I remember it was terminal four. Someone told us – I think maybe it was the pilot – to have our passports ready. I said to the agent, 'Where's my passport?' and he said, 'Don't worry.'

When we got to Passport Control there was an Indian guy checking passports. The agent went in front of me and mixed in with the other people, and I didn't see where he had gone: he had disappeared with my passport, so I had no ID with me. When the Asian guy asked me to show my passport, I told him the other guy had taken it, the one wearing a black jacket, but he didn't know who I was talking about.[18]

They took me to Immigration, and I explained what had happened. I told them my name was Hanes Abdulkadir, and that I was from Ethiopia and wanted to claim asylum. They brought the registration list for the plane, but I didn't know what name the agent had used on my passport, so they couldn't find me on the list. The interview took about one and a half hours. I spoke in broken English, but they didn't give me an interpreter.[19] The man who interviewed me was a good guy. He gave me a paper to sign for a solicitor, then I was taken to a hostel in Castle Green in London.

I met my solicitor and signed a form, which I had to take to the Home Office in Croydon within 15 days. I took it and got a receipt, but after a month they refused my claim because they said I had not handed the form in on time, but they were wrong, because my receipt was evidence. So I was refused without even having an interview.[20] Eventually, the judge admitted that they had made a mistake, but even so, I never had that initial interview. I have never had a chance to really explain why I came here – until today.

I was then moved to Salford, and in December 2002 my case went to a tribunal in Manchester. I still had not had an interview, so the judge just asked me a few questions. By then I had received letters from the Oromo Community in London and from the Head Office of the OLF in the USA. They confirmed my membership of the OLF, that I had been involved since 1999 and that they knew me personally.

Then in February 2003 I got the decision – another refusal. They said they did not believe that I was a member of the OLF because my letters were not from Ethiopia but from abroad. It wasn't what I expected. I was seeking sanctuary: I'm not a bogus asylum seeker. How could I get letters from Ethiopia, when the OLF was an illegal organisation there?[21] I'm still involved in politics for my people today. I go to demonstrations and meetings. Why would I do that after I had got my papers if I wasn't a genuine asylum seeker? I will be involved until the last day of my life. Some people have compromised their beliefs, but I will never compromise. Even a few days ago people were arrested in Ethiopia just for being Oromo. It was reported by Amnesty International.

I kept very active when I was waiting for my decision. I went to college to improve my English and went to meetings of my Oromo community in Manchester. Even when I got a negative decision, I didn't give up. I exercised and found a way to make myself useful. I put in a fresh asylum claim, and when the Home Office accepted it as a genuine claim, I was given Section 4 accommodation,[22] and vouchers for Asda supermarket.

For three years, from 2003 to 2006, I never had a reply about my fresh claim. I had the right to study, so I went to college and did my Business Studies Level 2. I also worked as a volunteer in the gallery at the Manchester University Museum with customer services. I still help out there sometimes.

It was such a difficult time waiting for that decision. It is a really stressful life, not knowing what is going to happen to you. It's not a life – you are left in limbo, without one penny in cash. Three years of living on vouchers. Sometimes I sold the vouchers, which were £30 a week, for £20, so I could have cash for things that you couldn't buy at Asda. Back then Asda didn't have as many things as they do today, like clothes.

At that time I was living in a house owned by a Pakistani guy. It was winter, around Christmas; there was no heater, and we didn't have a contact number for the owner. You can't live for two weeks over the holiday time with no heater in the house. I went to the shop to buy a heater, because Asda didn't sell them, and waited around to see if anyone would give me money for my vouchers. But some people would not believe that the vouchers were genuine, or that I would take £20 for them. Then one old lady stopped and went into Asda with me to check whether they were real. She gave me £25 for them, and I managed to buy a heater with that money.

Then in 2006 came my final refusal. I was on the street for almost a week until I met someone from the Ethiopian community who told me about the Boaz Trust. I went to the destitution project at St Bride's church, and there I met Dave Smith. The Boaz Trust was quite a small organisation back then. There were a lot of people on the waiting list for a house, and there was no room at the time. There were a lot of people needing somewhere, but you can't put ten people in a house.[23] That's not possible. So I came to pick up my food parcel and was back on the streets.

But the Boaz Trust soon found a room in a house in Moston for me. Nigel Biggs and his wife, Viv, came to pick me up and move me in. That's when my life began to change. Boaz didn't just give me accommodation. They gave me moral support and followed my case. I am a Muslim, but the Boaz Trust doesn't care what background you come from – only that you have a genuine case, that you are a genuine asylum seeker. It doesn't matter where you come from, only that you are destitute.

My life changed. First, I didn't have to worry about accommodation. I didn't have to worry about whether or not I would have something to eat. That was all sorted out. I had my first hot shower for a week. The house was nice. It was warm. For me, everything started from that time.

I started to go to classes at Boaz. It's not just about food and accommodation – you have to do something with your life. We're not like animals, just needing food and sleep. I went to computer classes and volunteered to run the Manchester 10k for Boaz. Having the 10k run as a goal motivated me to exercise for five months, and kept my mind on something – I would dream about the 10k![24] I also took part in the sleep-out for charity. Voluntary activities are important, so you're not sitting watching the telly every day.

The Boaz Trust changed many lives and stopped people going on drugs. It gives people the opportunity to do things, like W*, who is now in his first year at university. Even now we still think of the Boaz Trust as our family. If anything happens to us, we go to Boaz for help.

Some people I knew committed suicide when they were refused asylum, but I am a fighter. That is my strength. I believed in my case, so I didn't give up. Why should I? Boaz arranged for me to meet a solicitor at the North Manchester Law Centre, and I put in a fresh claim in 2009, but that was refused again.

One thing I haven't mentioned is that during all that time, for a whole ten years, I went to sign at the reporting centre every Monday. I complied with the Home Office. I never missed – not even one day. Then, one Monday in 2009, when I went to sign at Dallas Court, they detained me. First they took me to Manchester Airport;[25] then they took us overnight in a small car to a prison near Heathrow.[26] The car was full: I think there were eight or more people in it. It was cold, because it was winter. I couldn't feel my legs. A lady in the car asked them if she could go for a pee, but they wouldn't stop. There was no break from Manchester to London. There was nowhere to put your legs – how could you stay like that for four or five hours?

Then they lock you up, and they don't tell you anything – they make you very frustrated. In the middle of the night they come to you and say, 'Pack your stuff,' but they never tell you where you are going. I didn't know if I was going to London or Glasgow, or straight back to Ethiopia from the airport. The system is broken down; they just want to teach you a lesson.

It's like you are a criminal. I didn't commit any crime. There should have been open cells, but the way they treated us was not good. I think they do it to get you down, to teach you a lesson. They treat you like you're not supposed to be here, like you should go back home.

After two months I was transferred to Haslar IRC near Portsmouth. It used to be for youth offenders, but now it's used for deportations. I was there for two months as well. It was a much better place, with big grounds, where you can go running or take exercise. You aren't locked in the building like at Harmondsworth. I did computer classes while I was at Haslar.

While I was there they took me to the Ethiopian embassy, but the embassy refused to give me documents. I told them that I had never been granted Ethiopian citizenship, and that I had been against their policies ever since I have been here. Three weeks later the embassy wrote to the Home Office to say they didn't know me. Then I got bail: Dave was my surety, and they let me go back to Manchester to a Boaz house.

I was there for seven or eight months, and made another fresh claim, which was also refused, but then I got a letter from the Washington Office of the Oromo Liberation Front. The Home Office accepted the letter, and I was granted Section 4 accommodation in Bury.

Two months later I was called for an interview in Liverpool by the Home Office, but when I arrived there they said, 'Sorry, we made a mistake.[27] You've been refused.' My solicitor wrote to them, but she didn't get a reply. Then in September 2010 they wrote a letter to me to say that I was being granted leave to remain. I waited, and waited… they sent another letter asking for photographs… and I waited. Then I was asked to go to the Home Office to show all the activities and classes I had been doing since I came to the UK.

At that point Dave wrote to someone in the Home Office to ask what was going on. Finally, in February 2012 he got a letter back, asking for photographs again. We sent them, and five days later I got my papers. It was a final relief. I had been granted three years discretionary leave.

Now I am working full-time. I pay taxes like a citizen. I have never committed a crime and have never been taken to a police station. I respect the way of life of the British people. They are very lovely people. I left my country because I had a genuine problem. Ethiopia is still under a dictator. Even if I am a British citizen, I can't go home to visit my family. I would have to go to a neighbouring country.[28]

I got married last year, and my wife is expecting a baby. My life has changed. I have done my Level 3 in Business Studies and have been given a place at Salford University.

What are my dreams for the future? I want to work with a charity organisation in Africa, maybe even here. I want to reach my own people. It will be something to do with education. Where I come from, in the remote farming areas, people don't get any education. I want to go there, to bring them a pen and paper, to help children with their education, to found a humanitarian organisation. Education can change a future generation. Ethiopians can live as equals, side by side, with tolerance, respecting each other – that is my dream. It's not about independence; it's about people living together, side by side. That's what I have learned since coming to this country: people can live together. You can speak the Oromo language in your own land, or you can speak another language – it doesn't matter – but respect each other. That comes only from education, and there is no education in the remote areas of Ethiopia.

You know, I didn't expect things to happen like they did. People don't understand. I miss my country. I miss my family. I am of value to my people, but I was of no value here. For ten years I was not part of this society, but not part of my own people either. You are thrown out, and no one cares about you. You are not allowed to work; you are destitute. In history you learn about England, but the reality is different to that history. In England I have met many lovely people. In this country I am so proud, because I have freedom: I can say what I like. In my country I didn't have that freedom. Everything, all my political views, was controlled by the Ethiopian government; that's why I left.

I enjoy that freedom here; the freedom to speak my own language on the bus, for example. However, I never found that sanctuary I needed from UK government policy. Yes, there are a few bogus asylum seekers, but thousands of asylum seekers are like me: genuine asylum seekers who have been refused. The Home Office destroyed my life for ten years. I could have been a businessman, a community leader, but they took those ten years of my life, and I can never replace that time.

Reflections on Hanes' story

What would *you* do if you had to leave your country in a hurry? Where would you go? What would you take with you? How would you get across borders if you did not have a valid visa? Would you go to the nearest country and risk being found by your enemies, or go as far away as possible? How would you cope if you didn't speak the languages of the countries you passed through? Would your money last?

When Hanes set out for South Africa, it was a journey filled with uncertainty and fear. Things could have gone badly wrong at any stage. He could have been arrested before leaving Ethiopia, mugged and left for dead by traffickers, eaten by crocodiles, arrested by border police or beaten up by anti-immigrant groups. Those are all possible scenarios for the fleeing refugee, just as death by drowning in the Mediterranean or asphyxiation in the back of a sealed lorry might be.

Thankfully, Hanes has a strong will, and he survived to tell the tale. Many do not. He also survived the perils of the UK asylum system. Reading his story, you might be forgiven for thinking that 'system' is the wrong word for it, since in Hanes' case it appeared to work in a random and haphazard fashion, if it worked at all.

His story is indeed memorable, and it is, like all stories, unique, but is it unusual? In many ways his ordeal is typical of what the fleeing refugee has to endure. Those who have neither the resources nor the will to take the risks that he did are precisely those who, along with tens of thousands of others, spend years in miserably overcrowded refugee camps in a country next to their own.

Sadly, his experiences of the Home Office and the UK asylum system are not unusual either.

[3] According to the 2007 census, the population of Bale Robe was 44,382, but it was growing rapidly and had more than doubled since the previous census in 1994.

[4] The Oromo people are the largest ethnic grouping in Ethiopia, comprising 40-50 per cent of the population, yet they have very little representation in government.

[5] Amharic is the official working language of Ethiopia. It is the main language used in schools and is used in all official documents. The Oromo language, called Oromiffa, was until relatively recently banned from use in schools, despite being the language spoken at home by more than 20 million people.

[6] In 1974 Haile Selassie's government was replaced by the Derg, a military junta led by Mengistu Haile Mariam; but the Council was still Amhara-dominated, with only 25 non-Amhara members out of 125.

[7] 'The Oromo Liberation Front (OLF) is an organization established in 1973 by Oromo nationalists to promote self-determination for the Oromo people against "Abyssinian colonial rule". It was the culmination of over 70 years of uncoordinated resistance by Oromos against Amhara hegemony as well as oppression and suppression of the Oromo people and their culture. It has been outlawed and labeled a terrorist organization by the Ethiopian government. The OLF has offices in Asmara (military base), Washington D.C. and Berlin.' (https://en.wikipedia.org/wiki/Oromo_Liberation_Front (accessed 23rd March 2016))

[8] Menelik II, Emperor from 1889–1913.

[9] The current Ethiopian government of the Ethiopian People's Revolutionary Democratic Front (EPRDF) is dominated by members of the Tigrayan People's Liberation Front (TPLF). Other groups, especially the Oromo, are marginalised.

[10] When people ask, 'Why don't they just go to the next country?' this is one of the main reasons. Government spies are plentiful, and it is difficult for refugees to trust anyone from their own country.

[11] Jatani Ali Tandhu (1939–1992) was the leader of the Borana Oromo people and former provincial governor of Borana province in southern Ethiopia. He was shot dead in Nairobi in 1992.

[12] Inflation in Mozambique had climbed to around 25 per cent by early 2002, and one US dollar was worth around 23,000 meticals.

[13] Known as *ugali* in Kenya and Tanzania, it is a starchy, porridge-like mush made from cornmeal, often used as a side dish. The South African name for it is *pap* or *mealie pap*.

[14] The African National Congress (ANC) is the Republic of South Africa's governing social democratic political party. It has been the ruling party of post-apartheid South Africa since 1994.

[15] As the political and economic situation worsened in neighbouring countries, particularly Zimbabwe, many people fled to South Africa. Between 2000 and March 2008, at least 67 people died in what were identified as xenophobic attacks. In May 2008, a series of anti-immigrant riots left 62 people dead.

[16] In order to get out of their country, most asylum seekers have to have a false passport: it is impossible to apply for a genuine one if they are wanted by their government.

[17] This is typical of agents. They often have legitimate businesses in the UK, and trafficking is a lucrative sideline.

[18] Agents do not want to be caught. They keep hold of the false passports and disappear soon after arrival.

[19] Asylum seekers are entitled to an interpreter at their screening interview.

[20] This was clearly a breach of Home Office procedures. Every asylum seeker is entitled to a substantive interview.

[21] This is the catch-22 for political asylum seekers. If you try to get documents from the organisation in your own country, you endanger those you ask to send them. If you get them from the overseas headquarters of the organisation, the Home Office places little or no value on them.

[22] Section 4 accommodation now consists of shared accommodation (which can be anywhere in the UK) and £35.39 a week via an 'Azure' payment card which can be used at major supermarkets, Boots the Chemist and a few charity shops. There is no cash support. It is given primarily to those whose fresh claims are accepted as having merit, while the claim is considered. Critics believe it is deliberately harsh, in order to force people to leave the UK. The government is planning to phase it out, but there are grave concerns among refugee groups that this will lead to even more destitution than at present.

[23] In theory it would be possible to cram more people in, but only at the risk of causing friction and more stress. Everyone has the right to a safe space they can call their own, even if it's only a small bedroom.

[24] Hanes is The Boaz Trust's fastest ever 10k runner! He even got to meet the world-famous Ethiopian runner, Haile Gebreselassie, winner of the Manchester 10k, when being interviewed at the BBC studios before the event.

[25] Pennine House is the Holding Centre for up to ten people at Manchester Airport. You can be held there for up to five days before being transferred to an Immigration Removal Centre (IRC).

[26] Harmondsworth IRC.

[27] I guess at least they said sorry for their mistake, though that is hardly a consolation. It was not the only 'mistake' made in Hanes' case. There were multiple administrative errors, compounded by a presumption that he was not telling the truth.

[28] In January 2016 Hanes applied for a travel document from the Home Office to go to see his sick mother. Because he still fears returning to Ethiopia, he intended to meet her in a neighbouring country. The Home Office refused, saying that, since they had not granted him asylum but only given him discretionary leave, they did not accept that he could not go to the Ethiopian embassy and get an Ethiopian passport. They also kept the fee he paid, which they said was 'non-returnable'.

Ayesha's* story

I was born in 1970 in Al Fashir, the capital city of North Darfur in north-western Sudan. My parents were from an Arab tribe called the Rizeigat[29] who lived in that part of the country alongside the black African Darfuri tribes. My father was a cattle trader, like many Rizeigat tribesman, and my mother was a teacher.

When I was five years old we moved to Omdurman.[30] There are three large cities together, which make up Khartoum: Khartoum proper is the political centre and capital city of Sudan, Khartoum Bahri is the industrial centre, and Omdurman is like the cultural capital of Sudan: together they make up Khartoum. My mother wanted to move to Omdurman to teach in a primary school.

I grew up there with my parents, my sister and my brother. I am the oldest child. I started primary school at six years of age and went on to secondary school and high school[31] until I was ready to apply for university. It was a difficult time for the family because my father was very involved politically. He was a communist, but the communist party was forbidden during Nimeiry's time in Sudan.[32] He was often interrogated, imprisoned and beaten. He was in prison three times.

I got a scholarship to go to university, and my parents sent me to Russia to study medicine. I was there for seven years – one year studying Russian and six studying medicine. I spent two years in Moscow, then went to Yalta on the Black Sea. While I was there my dad passed away, so I came back to live with my family. I got a job as a trainee doctor at Khartoum Hospital. I had to do two years training to be a general practitioner. There was no specialisation like there is in the UK. You automatically become a general practitioner at the end of the two years.

After training you had to do two years in rural hospitals. You could choose where you went. They needed doctors in the hospitals in Darfur, so I applied to go there, and they accepted me. I worked for a while in the hospital in Al Fashir, and also for a while in a very small hospital in Kurdufan. I wasn't working in one fixed place: they moved me where they needed me.

At that time the war in Darfur had already started, but it wasn't that bad. After a while the situation got much worse. The Sudanese army started bombing the area around Al Fashir. They couldn't come directly into the capital, but they attacked the rebels in the rural areas nearby. We started to see people brought into the hospital with gunshot wounds, and many women and girls who had been raped by the Janjaweed.[33] In the west of Sudan there are tribes of pure African origin and tribes of Arab origin. The Janjaweed are Arab tribes working with the government, who arm them to fight against local tribes of African origin. Everyone knows it happens, but it's not done openly. It's a conspiracy that's done 'under the table'.

At the beginning of the war the government was controlling Al Fashir, but it became a mess really. They started to gradually evacuate the doctors who were on the side of the government. There was a group of us who were left. I can't say that we were really anti-government, but the government didn't like what we were doing.

At that time there were some foreign human rights groups in Sudan, like Oxfam and Save the Children, and also a Sudanese human rights group linked to Amnesty, who were trying to expose what was really going on – all the rapes, the atrocities and the torture. The government was trying to cover up what was happening. I and some of my colleagues decided to start helping one of the groups by collecting reports on women and children from the hospitals, as well as our personal reports on the people we were treating. We decided to pass the information on to the Sudanese human rights group, but it was difficult at that time to make contact with them. It was very dangerous. They were based in Khartoum, and we had no direct contact with them; we just knew some of their names, but they had supporters among the elders in various tribes who were respected by the people, like the sheikhs and imams.

I worked closely with three other doctors, all men. We tried to keep the group small for safety reasons. All of the information we collected was regularly given to a sheikh from the Rizeigat tribe, and he passed it on to the human rights group. He was someone I had known for a long time, as he was a friend of my father, and very well known by everyone as the head of the tribe.

After a while the security forces,[34] who were everywhere, found out what we were doing. They are part of the army, but similar to the Soviet Union's KGB. They arrested me and two of my colleagues. They interrogated us. They wanted to know the names of the people we were passing the information on to, and which other doctors were involved. I couldn't give them any information because I didn't know about the other people, only the doctors in my group and the sheikh, and they already knew about him. I wasn't really tortured physically; it was more like psychological torture.

After about a month of being locked up in a room in their headquarters they told us that they would release us if we signed a document to say we would no longer work in this area. They told me to go back to Khartoum. They threatened to kill us if we didn't sign, so I signed, and went back to live with my mum and siblings in Khartoum. When I got there I found I was on a government blacklist, so I couldn't get my old job back in the hospital, and I couldn't get any other jobs either. Every time I applied for a job they made an excuse: there wasn't a vacancy; I would have to wait. There were all sorts of unacceptable excuses. From time to time the security police would do something to try to disturb me: they would be watching the house, following me wherever I went. They even searched the house a couple of times. That wasn't new: they had done that many times when my father was alive.

My brother had also been in trouble with the authorities a few times because he was a communist like my dad, though he was never put in prison. My sister was OK because she got married and moved away. She was never involved anyway. My mum was worried about me, and she encouraged me to leave the country. I couldn't work anyway, so I started to make plans to get out.

I already had a passport, which I had needed to study in Russia, but it had expired. When I wanted to renew it, there was a problem, because they wouldn't let doctors leave the country unless they had done military service or were over the age of 40. This was in 2005, and I was only 35 years old, so I had to get the age changed on my passport in order to get out. Corruption is everywhere in Africa, so it was really easy to do that. You just have to pay a lot of money.

I had got to know a British lady when I was working in Darfur. She was working in administration for an NGO. She knew a Sudanese doctor working in the UK. He was a surgeon in Bournemouth. The lady contacted the Sudanese doctor, and he was willing to take responsibility for me, so he offered me a three-month clinical placement. He sent a letter to the British embassy, which the lady said was the only way I was going to be able to get a valid visa for the UK. When I had got my passport I went to the embassy, and it was really quite easy to get the visa.

The real problem was getting through the airport: because my passport had been changed, anything could have happened. We chose a flight during the night, and bribed the duty officer in charge of the night shift to let me through. He had to know I was coming and pay those working under him to let me through, so it was expensive: altogether it cost millions.[35] It was also quite frightening because I could have been arrested at any time as I was passing through.

I arrived in the UK at Heathrow Airport on 29th November 2005. It was much colder than Sudan, but I was used to it because I had lived in Russia! The good thing was that I was able to bring my medical and educational certificates with me, so I could prove my qualifications. I just had basic English, which I had learned in school. I didn't get a chance to study English when I was in Russia, so it was difficult at the beginning.

At first I stayed with a friend of my father, who lived in Huddersfield. We had already arranged this, so he knew I was coming. Then I contacted the doctor in Bournemouth and went to see him, but I never actually did my clinical placement. I just wanted to go and say thank you. He tried to persuade me to do the placement, but I wasn't ready to do that. I was confused and told him I needed to sort out my life first.

I went back to stay with my father's friend. I didn't apply for asylum straight away. I had to get things clear in my mind and become calm before I was ready to do that. He helped me to apply after about two months in the UK. I had to go to the Home Office in Liverpool for the screening interview. After I applied for asylum, the Home Office sent me to live in Bradford.

After about two or three months I had to go to Liverpool again for my first interview.[36] Because of stress, I was having problems with my periods and was bleeding heavily. The Home Office had sent me a ticket to get to Liverpool and put me up in a hotel for the night because my interview was early the next morning. However, during the night I started to bleed heavily and had to call for an ambulance. They took me to hospital, where I stayed for three days, so I missed my interview. I went back to Bradford, and the Home Office didn't call me for another interview until the end of 2006, so it was almost a whole year before I had my initial interview.

I was quite lucky really, because there weren't so many asylum seekers in Bradford at that time. I was given a one-bedroom flat on my own. I didn't know how to go about things back then, about going to school to learn English, or anything. There was no Sudanese community in Bradford, and it was six months before I met a Sudanese lady there. She was also an asylum seeker, and she introduced me to some other Sudanese, but it wasn't a big community.

I did have some friends: one girl from Ethiopia and one from Uganda. I spent most of my time with them. I didn't bring much money with me from Sudan, but I managed OK, because I wasn't going anywhere or doing anything much. I felt very isolated and confused because I didn't know what was going on, and everything was new for me. The Ethiopian girl helped and supported me because she had been here for three or four years, but no one else helped me much.

I also knew a man in Manchester, who told me about an organisation called Reache,[37] which is a medical charity for refugee doctors. I applied, but they told me they only accepted people who lived near Manchester because it is difficult to commute. I wrote a letter to the Home Office to tell them about this, and that I wanted to move to Manchester, and they accepted this. They sent me to Salford, where I shared a two-bedroomed flat with another asylum seeker.

I was eventually called for my initial interview late in 2006. It only lasted about two hours. I was interviewed by a man. What I remember about the interview was that he was always making out that I was lying, and was always asking for evidence, always evidence. I told him frankly, 'I don't have any evidence except my certificates.' He didn't believe that I had worked in Darfur, and wanted proof that I had worked in the hospital in Al Fashir, but how could I get that evidence? The hospital in Al Fashir is run by the government – they would not give me a letter to prove I had been there.

He wanted me to prove everything, but you can't get that evidence – it's difficult. The government was not going to help me get it, and there was no one else who could. You can't send for it, and even if you get it, then they question you about *how* you got it.[38]

He even wanted copies of the documents I gave to the sheikh, but I didn't keep any copies for security reasons, obviously. And he wanted names of the contacts in Amnesty, but I never had direct contact with anyone there. He also kept saying that it was safe to live in Khartoum, so I could go back there. He said it would be safe to relocate.[39]

At first I had a solicitor in Bradford, who was quite good, but then I had to change to one in Manchester, who didn't seem very bothered about my case. I was actually expecting my appeal to be refused. I honestly can't remember when I was refused. All the dates are mixed up in my head. I think I was refused maybe three times: first of all when I had my solicitor in Bradford, then my appeal was refused when I was with the law centre in Longsight in Manchester. I also had a solicitor in London; I think that was before the one in Longsight.[40] Raj [41] did a judicial review[42] for me, but that was refused. Then I contacted RAPAR.[43]

When I was with my London solicitor, I told him that I was so fed up that I wanted to go home. I asked him to write to the Home Office and tell them that. He asked me if I was sure that I wanted to do that, and I said, 'Yes, I'm fed up,' so he wrote to the Home Office, but they ignored the letter for a year – they didn't reply. When they did eventually reply, they asked me to start signing at the reporting centre.[44] Up to then they hadn't told me to do that. In the letter they didn't mention anything about going back to Sudan or getting a passport. I had to sign at the centre every week.

I was in Salford for two years. During that time I was able to attend Reache, but after my appeal had been refused, I had to stop going there. I couldn't manage financially when they stopped my support, and I was not in the right mood to study. If you are not settled and relaxed, you can't study because you can't concentrate.[45]

I also had to leave my accommodation. I stayed with a male friend for maybe two years, but it wasn't comfortable. At first he tried to help me, but after a while he took advantage of me and my situation, because I had nowhere to go. He started to abuse me. I was so disappointed, and pretty depressed. The whole situation was very stressful.[46]

Then an Ethiopian lady told me about the Red Cross.[47] I went there, but was still living with that guy because they didn't have accommodation. It was horrible at that time, honestly. After one year they referred me to the Boaz Trust. That's when I got a place to live, and everything was OK for me. I was in a shared house in Rusholme with an Ethiopian lady and some others; then I was moved to another house nearby. I think I was there for about three years.

It's enough that Boaz gave me a place, where I could close the door and say, 'This is my place.' A place where I could sleep, feel safe and no one would bother me, where there was no boyfriend, nobody to take advantage of me. That was the most important thing.

The second thing was getting help: money, food, different activities – and the feeling that somebody cares about you, that they want to know what your problem is. You know where you can go if you have a problem and who you can talk to, and you are 100 per cent sure there will be a solution. That's a big thing really. You know from Boaz that you can take without giving. They are willing to give. With other people everything is conditional. They won't help you just like that. If you want something, you have to give something.

When I was with Boaz I volunteered in the Mustard Tree[48] shop. I did four years there in customer service, and some short courses. It gave me a new perspective on things that I never thought I would come across in my life. It was good, a new experience for me, working with those sorts of vulnerable people. It was different from working in a hospital. It has also helped me when I apply for other sorts of jobs now.

I was also involved at WAST.[49] I can't forget them – you feel like family there. I don't want to disconnect from them. I was with them when I was an asylum seeker. You share your problems with them and they help you. Now I am volunteering with them every Friday if I am not working. It is good to socialise and to have time for relaxation. I still go singing with them.

RAPAR found me a solicitor in London, and he started working on a fresh claim for me. At that time I was still living in the Boaz house in Rusholme. I went to sign one Wednesday at the reporting centre, and they detained me. It happened so suddenly that it was really a shock. I wasn't expecting it, because I had an appointment in Liverpool with the Home Office four or five days later to hand in my fresh claim. My solicitor had already sent in the fresh claim, but they sent it back, saying that they had changed the rules, and I now had to hand it in in person, in Liverpool.

When they detained me, I called my boyfriend, Mazir, and he came and brought my medication from my house. He called my solicitor and my friends and also went to tell the staff in the Boaz office.

When they took me to detention at Yarl's Wood,[50] they sent all of my file to my previous solicitor, not my current solicitor. When Mazir contacted my solicitor, the solicitor told him he hadn't received anything from the Home Office. They had messed up. After that they did send the documents to the right place.

I wasn't in detention for long, about five days, but it was like hell really. I wasn't expecting it, and it was something new for me: the way they took me, and forced me to go to my embassy. They handcuffed me, and gave my passport to the officer at the embassy. Really, it was very humiliating. I didn't want to go, but they told me that if I didn't it would be bad for me. I asked them how they could take me to my embassy when I was asking for asylum, but they just said it was their orders, and they didn't know anything about my case.

The embassy asked me everything about where I lived, about my family, everything about home. Apparently they had been asked by the Home Office to renew my passport. I was in the embassy for about three hours, and then they took me back to detention. I don't know what happened about the embassy after that. No one said anything.

On the fifth day at about seven o'clock in the morning a guy came to my cell and told me, 'You are free to go.' He handed me a ticket, and took me in a car to the train station. My solicitor had written to them to say that it was an unlawful detention, because I had an appointment for a fresh claim and a case in process.[51]

After that I applied for Section 4,[52] and that was accepted, so I was given accommodation in Hyde. There really wasn't anything much that was new in my fresh claim, only my relationship with Mazir. I had become a Christian[53] in 2011, and I know that was another reason why they couldn't send me back, but I didn't *want* that to be the reason: I believed I already had a good case.

After about seven or eight months the Home Office wrote to my solicitor to clarify some points. He interviewed me over the phone. They asked the same questions, and I gave the same answers. There were about 20 questions. Nothing was any different. About two weeks later I got my papers, eight years after I applied for asylum.

You know, when your life is on hold you go through so much stress and depression. You become numb really. Even when I got my status, I can't say I was so happy about it, and I can't say I was surprised. I didn't know *what* I was feeling when I heard for the first time. I was just confused and shocked. People are playing with your life and they destroy you from inside.

When you get your status, your life is already ruined. It's so difficult to get yourself together and start a new, fresh life. It's *so* difficult. You can't just leave everything behind: there's a scar there. There *is* hope though, otherwise there is no meaning in life. Suddenly you find yourself turned round 180 degrees. It's a big shift. You had a problem, and now you have a new problem: how to adapt to the new system, you know.

You have to depend on yourself now. When you are an asylum seeker, you have support, but when you get your papers, you are on your own. You still don't understand how things work, like how to apply for a job at the Job Centre; it's really difficult.

I was lucky really, because Boaz was still supporting me. Olwen still supported me too.[54] So did Mazir, who got his status a long time before me. So I had support, but it was still difficult. Slowly, slowly I am getting there – slowly, slowly. I am still in contact with my family, and am planning to meet them in Egypt or Ethiopia, but first I need to work and get some money.

The thing that I have most suffered from, and still do, is that I lost my confidence, and can't practice as a doctor. Eight years is a long time not practicing, and I wonder if I will ever practise again. I am trying, but I can't concentrate: I can't remember – my memory is ruined. When I studied medicine, and medicine is the most difficult subject to study, I did well. I even had to study it in a foreign language, not my own language. And I did work as a doctor, but these eight years have taken a lot out of me. Now I am hesitant. I am not sure I can do the exam. I have no confidence. Medicine is the only thing I know. It is my career, and I don't want to regret ... but these eight years ... they took a lot out of me.

Life here is very fast, and the system is totally different from what I am used to back home. You know what drives me crazy? It's the letters: letters from the Job Centre, letters from Manchester Council, letters from everywhere – it's just crazy and confusing.[55] The Job Centre is a nightmare. First of all, they don't care that you are doing training to try and get into your career. All they want is for you to search for a job, to do a full-time job. Some of them understand and try to help, but it's their job at the end of the day. There are so many appointments. They send you to work programmes, and then, when you get stuck, they try to force you to do all kinds of jobs – cleaning ... any kind of job. I told them that I don't mind doing some sort of job until I finish my study and do my exam; even a full-time job, I don't mind.

But then there is another problem. When you apply for a job, they don't reply, or they need experience, or they don't accept you because you are a foreigner – it's so difficult! Sometimes when they show you a job or you find it on the website, you don't even understand the job title. They are such long titles and fancy names, and you think, 'What's this job about?' Honestly, sometimes I just don't understand. It might be a normal job that you could apply for, but nobody explains what it means.[56]

I have finished my studies now. Now it's just repetition and revision. The exam is in two months. I want to try the exam; I want to give it a go, but I'm not sure about it. At the moment I am doing medical translation in Arabic in a hospital. It's not far from my career, but it's not the job that I want.

What does the future hold? I don't know. I'm not young. I'm getting old, and I *feel* that deep inside me. I feel like I am older than I really am. I am so exhausted. I am tired, and now I feel the effects of those eight years. I feel the heaviness. Sometimes I just want to relax and do nothing, but that's not living. I need to do something.

You discover new things in yourself when you go through experiences like this. You discover new qualities inside you. You are human, and you have your weaknesses, but you have to be really strong to survive all these problems. It's a good lesson to learn. They say, 'What doesn't kill you makes you stronger.' I think that's definitely true.

Listening to Ayesha's story

At first it was fairly easy to understand Ayesha's story – until she started talking about the asylum process that she went through. At that point it became increasingly difficult to work out exactly what had gone on, and I had to keep asking for clarification. 'When was that? Which solicitor was it? Do you mean the initial interview or the appeal? Were you in Bradford or Salford when that happened?'

It was as if dates, times and the order of events had become jumbled, thoughts and feelings confused and some things totally forgotten. As Ayesha said herself at one point, 'I honestly can't remember when I was refused. All the dates are mixed up in my head.'

Sorting out the order and details of events was not easy. In fact, I'm still not sure whether it's all in the right order, but to be quite honest, a neat and orderly account would have been at the expense of understanding how Ayesha's life was messed up by a rigid, inflexible asylum system and the mistakes of those who administer it. The messiness of that part of her story is testimony to that.

What fascinates me most is that the part of Ayesha's story that was hardest to recall was not her arrest and persecution in Sudan, but her time in the UK asylum system. It is as if *that* was far more stressful, and therefore more in need of being blotted out, than anything suffered at the hands of the Sudanese security forces. [57]

Eight years is a long time to lose from a life, but perhaps, with the lessons that she has learned through her suffering and her new faith in a good God, her future will yet be a glorious one. After all, the God of the Bible is the one who promises: 'I will restore to you the years that the swarming locust has eaten' (Joel 2:25, NKJV).

---

[29] The Rizeigat are a Muslim and Arabic tribe of the nomadic Bedouin people, most of whom live in south-east Darfur. The Rizeigat are the largest and most powerful of the Baggara Arab people in Darfur. The Northern Rizeigat herd camels and the Southern Rizeigat herd cattle.
[30] 'Omdurman is the largest city in Sudan and Khartoum State, lying on the western banks of the River Nile, opposite the capital, Khartoum. It has a population of 2,395,159 (2008) and is the national centre of

commerce' (https://en.wikipedia.org/wiki/Omdurman (accessed 23rd March 2016)).

[31] Primary education in Sudan is free and compulsory for children aged 6 to 13, followed by three years of secondary education. Attendance of primary age pupils is around 53 per cent. Around two-thirds of those who complete primary school go on to secondary education. Figures for high school and university are hard to find.

[32] On May 25, 1969 the Sudanese government was overthrown in a military coup led by Gaafar Nimeiry. In 1971 the Sudanese Communist Party (SCP) led a *coup d'état* which failed. The leaders of the coup were executed and the SCP suppressed.

[33] The Janjaweed are Arab tribesmen who have been armed by the Sudanese government and encouraged to suppress black African tribes such as those in Darfur by destroying villages, stealing property and livestock, and raping women.

[34] The Sudanese security forces have been responsible for thousands of human rights violations in the past few years: a brief online search quickly reveals the extent of atrocities routinely carried out against their own citizens.

[35] Ayesha can't remember exactly how much money changed hands for the passport and safe passage. 250 Sudanese Dinars were worth about one US dollar in 2005, so her assertion that it was 'millions' is likely to be accurate, as a million dinars would be the equivalent of $4,000, and false documents alone often cost more than that.

[36] The substantive interview. This is the main interview, after which a decision to grant or refuse asylum is made.

[37] Reache (Refugee and Asylum Seekers Centre for Healthcare Professionals Education) North West assists refugee and asylum-seeking Healthcare Professionals (RHPs) to register their qualifications in the UK. It has an education centre in Salford Royal NHS Foundation Trust. It also assists RHPs who have permission to work in seeking professional employment in the NHS. More information can be found at www.reache.wordpress.com (accessed 23rd March 2016).

[38] This is another catch-22 situation. The Home Office insists on proof, therefore documents are required, but once the documents are obtained they often argue that they are fakes.

[39] The Home Office regularly tells asylum seekers that they will be safe in another part of the country. In Ayesha's case that is patently untrue, because she fled from Khartoum, where she was on a government blacklist. She would not have been able to practise medicine anywhere in Sudan.

[40] At this point Ayesha was trying hard to remember the order in which things happened, but had real difficulty in doing so. The whole experience of seeking asylum had evidently been so stressful that, when it was over, she had shut much of it out from her memory. Clearly she did not *want* to remember the wasted years in her life.

[41] Raj Brightman, from Scott Moncrieff solicitors, London, began working with Boaz as an immigration solicitor in 2011. Over the years he has been a real blessing to many clients, bringing hope where there was none. He looks at the cases of Boaz clients who are not already represented, and takes on their cases wherever possible. This has led to many refused asylum seekers being granted refugee status.

[42] A judicial review can only be made when there has been an error in law.

[43] RAPAR is a Manchester-based human rights organisation working with displaced people facing challenges relating to citizenship, housing, deportation, employment, education, personal safety and other problems (http://www.rapar.org.uk (accessed 23rd March 2016)).

[44] Asylum seekers, whether still in the system or after refusal, are usually required to report (or sign, the term used in the sector) regularly at an Immigration Reporting Centre – in this case, Dallas Court in Salford (see note 137). It appears that the Home Office had omitted to tell Ayesha to do this.

[45] Many intelligent and determined asylum seekers are in the middle of a college course when their appeal is refused. Although they are allowed to stay on until the end of that term or module, in practice it is difficult to do so. With nowhere permanent to live and no money for fares to get to college, it is a real struggle to continue, and even if they manage to do so, their ability to concentrate is severely affected by their circumstances and uncertain future.

[46] Female asylum seekers are often pressurised into relationships which they would otherwise not consider, simply because they have nowhere else to go. It's often more complicated than 'sex for a bed',

but the bottom line is that destitution forces them into unwanted sexual relationships.

For a comprehensive overview of what destitute asylum seekers do to survive, read the report 'Coping with Destitution', Oxfam, Feb 2011, (http://policy-practice.oxfam.org.uk/publications/coping-with-destitution-survival-and-livelihood-strategies-of-refused-asylum-se-121667 (accessed 23rd March 2016)).

[47] The Red Cross Destitution Project at St. Bride's Church in Old Trafford. Refused asylum seekers can access a food parcel and a bus fare for up to a year after being made destitute, as well as advice and signposting to other services. This was the first asylum destitution project in the UK, and has been running since 2003.

[48] Mustard Tree is a charity based in Manchester for the homeless and marginalised. It offers cheap second-hand clothes, furniture and household items in its shop, and a range of courses and volunteering opportunities to get people back on their feet and into employment (http://www.mustardtree.org.uk (accessed 23rd March 2016)).

[49] Women Asylum Seekers Together (WAST) is a Manchester-based self-help group for women asylum seekers under threat of deportation. It provides a safe and secure women-only space and they can be a source of social and emotional support for each other (http://www.wast.org.uk (accessed 23rd March 2016)).

[50] Yarl's Wood is an Immigration Removal Centre for women near Bedford. It is run by Serco, which has been heavily criticised for its failure to provide adequate medical treatment and protection for its inmates from sexist and racist male guards. In March 2015 an undercover investigation from Channel 4 exposed the abuses (http://www.channel4.com/news/yarls-wood-immigration-removal-detention-centre-investigation (accessed 23rd March 2016)).

In August 2015 *The Independent* published a report that showed that conditions there had worsened for detainees in the past year (http://www.independent.co.uk/news/uk/crime/yarls-wood-conditions-at-immigration-removal-centre-have-deteriorated-so-much-that-female-detainees-10450554.html (accessed 23rd March 2016)).

[51] A great deal of money is wasted detaining people who are about to put in a fresh claim for asylum. It should not be too difficult for the reporting centre to check with the asylum seeker's solicitor before setting the detention wheels in motion.

[52] See footnote 22.

[53] Ayesha said this of her conversion from Islam: 'When I met Mazir, he tried to introduce me to Christianity, but it's difficult when you have been brought up in Islam, and it took a long time for me to convince myself. I was baptised, and two months later I got my status. I feel freer now, and it gave me a kind of peace. Islam is all about fear. Everything is forbidden, not allowed ... if you don't do things you will be punished ... everything is conditional. A lot of people – not all of them – do things because it's cultural, not because they believe. Islam and culture are mixed together, like wearing the hijab, or fasting, or going to the mosque. But Christianity is totally different. I don't believe in Catholic and Protestant and all these sub-divisions. I just believe in Jesus. He has the way. Christianity is a lifestyle. I follow His way.'

[54] Olwen Ridyard ran the sewing class at Boaz for many years, providing respite and friendship for many of the female clients (as well as an occasional male or two). Classes like this are so important to make those with so much time on their hands feel valued.

[55] This is where friends can make a huge difference, especially British friends. Refugee organisations do their best to provide advice and to help refugees cope with their sudden new life, but cannot replace genuine friends, who can sit down over a cup of coffee and help them to deal with things like bills, utilities, council tax and benefits.

[56] One of the greatest needs for those who have been granted refugee status is help to navigate the system. Even those like Ayesha, who have good English, struggle to understand what to do. Those with little English find it impossible to comply with Job Centre requirements and often end up being sanctioned as a result. It would be hugely cost effective to employ one or two specialist staff in each Job Centre to deal with immigrants.

[57] The Centre for the Study of Emotion and Law (CSEL) has produced some excellent studies on the effect of trauma on the memory. In 2012 they published a toolkit for those working with asylum-seeking women. As I was reading through the section on indicators of post-traumatic stress, I was able to identify several that were present in Ayesha – all of which could be attributed to the stress encountered since her arrival in the UK, not before. Apart from persistent depression, these are clearly also present:

- inability to recall an important aspect of the trauma
- feelings of detachment or distance
- a loss of a sense of future.

(http://www.csel.org.uk/assets/images/resources/training-toolkit-2012-csel/CSEL-toolkit-final-web-august2012.pdf (accessed 23rd March 2016)).

Maron's story

I was born in January 1971, in Wembo-Nyama in Kasai-Oriental in central Democratic Republic of Congo. My parents are originally from Lubefu and settled in Wembo-Nyama where my dad was the headmaster in a Methodist church school. I was born a Christian in a typical Methodist church. I remember that on Sunday we were not allowed to do any activities except play. There was no work to do. Everyone went to church. My early life was slightly different from many people because I was born into a family of nine. I was the fourth child. My dad's dad was king in the lower kingdom of Ngandu, and we had a domestic helper at home to do all the cooking, washing and ironing.

My dad was supposed to be his father's successor, but he opted to go into education instead. In the Congo you have to pay to go to nursery or primary school, and my dad was really keen to support anyone who was willing to learn, so he often paid their fees. He also paid for some who were bright but about to drop out because their parents couldn't afford to pay for their education.

I went to primary school in Onalua, which was the village that Patrice Lumumba[58] came from. I actually spent a lot of time playing with Lumumba's younger brother before I started primary school, but of course I didn't know who he was at that time. My favourite place to play was near the small monument that was erected after he was killed.

At secondary school, the system was that you had to choose what subjects you wanted to do at about age 13 or 14. I opted for biology, because I wanted to go into medicine. I also excelled at physics and maths, so I was put in for the exams at 18 in all four sciences: maths, physics, chemistry and biology. After I passed, they asked me to teach. I did one year teacher training (child and adolescent pedagogy), then started teaching physics, mathematics, chemistry and English.

My childhood was very happy. My dad was very structured and strict. At mealtimes we were told to take only what we wanted to eat, and there was a time to study and a time for play. He spent time with us, helping with our studies. When I was 13 or 14 a group of Americans came over as missionaries – Tom and Kay Fleming and their children, Adam, Aaron and Bethany. I became good friends with the children, and they wanted me to live with them, but my dad wasn't keen: he thought I might drop off in my studies. At that time I was living in one of the two small houses in the compound next to our big house. The other one was for guests. We also had two rooms for guests in the big house. Sometimes we would take in, free of charge, students who had nowhere to stay, and who had too far to walk to school from where they lived, up to 100 km away in Katako Kombe. At weekends they would go back to their families.

The Flemings invited me to go to the United States with them, but my dad didn't want us to go too far away. I already had one older brother studying in Kinshasa, and one in Kisangani, and my dad had become quite protective of us and worried if we were away for a long time.

I first became aware of political things when I was 17. I remember going on a trip to Onalua, which was just seven kilometres away, with my American friends, Aaron and Adam. When we got there we took a lot of photos near Lumumba's monument. I didn't really know who Lumumba was, but if you mentioned his name back then you would have got arrested and taken to Makala prison, as if it was an attempt to bring down Mobutu's regime.

When we got back home, Tom (the American missionary) said to me, 'Jim,[59] you know, someone as bright as you would be driving an expensive car back in the US.'

I asked, 'What makes us different from the US?' and he reminded me of the time I had been banned from church for wearing a tie. I was just dressing like my American friends, but one of Mobutu's[60] rules was that no Congolese was allowed to wear a tie.[61] This was abolished on 30th April 1990. That led to talking about Lumumba, and I realised what an important guy he had been. Later on I found out that my dad had a photo of Lumumba that he had buried in our house. He checked on it on a yearly basis. If they had found out, he would have been taken to prison and killed. Mobutu travelled everywhere in the Congo, but never came to Lubefu or Katako, which is where Lumumba was born. I think he kept a stricter eye on that area though.

After teacher training I decided to go to university at Kisangani to study medicine. Tom and Aaron had gone back to the US by then. My dad wasn't very happy about my decision, as he thought I was too far away to get any financial support to me if I needed it, but I wanted to be away from home so I would be independent and not rely on our domestic helper all the time. I had a friend from college in Wembo called Daniel Pongo who was already studying at Kisangani University. We spent most of our time studying or doing research at the French Cultural Centre there.

Towards the end of my time Mobutu planned to come to make an official speech in Kisangani. It was 24th November 1993.[62] Most students felt that he was not welcome, because students had recently been massacred in Lubumbashi[63] and attacked in Kinshasa. We didn't want to take part in the singing and dancing and stuff: he wasn't popular any more because of the attacks on students. The administrative office of our university ordered all students to attend. We knew that they would clamp down and dismiss students who did not attend, so we planned to attend and 'boo' him instead of clapping. That was something that no one had dared to do before in Congo. When that happened on the day there were clashes with the army, who came from Lubunga on the left bank of river Congo in Kisangani. We retreated and went home. I told Daniel that I didn't want to stay around because the DSP[64] were out in the fields. We were preparing to go back to uni in the morning, but we went to stay with Daniel's aunt that evening in Kabondo, equivalent of a borough in Kisangani.

71

During the night soldiers came from Lubunga and attacked students. They didn't go with guns, but they slashed everything with swords and cordellettes (special wires normally used to climb walls). In the morning we went to get a bus to go to the campus, but when we got there everything was closed. There were five burned-out buses. They blamed that on the students. There was blood everywhere in the dormitories, and slashed mattresses, but no one knew who had been killed or who had got away because there were no corpses left. Then the soldiers came back armed just with their cordellettes and challenged the students to fight. It was mad: a street fight in the middle of the town.

I phoned my uncle in Kinshasa, and he told me to get out. It would have been dangerous to go by plane or by road, because they would be checking. I was out walking in the evening with two friends, and we were stopped by soldiers. They said, 'You three are students.' We denied it, but they said again, 'You three are students.'

So we said, 'Where did you see us studying?'

Then they said, 'Your French sounds like you are students,' but they let us go.

My uncle in Kinshasa contacted another 'uncle', a distant relative, who was a colonel in the army at Kisangani, and explained my situation. I went to see him, and he wrote a letter saying that I was his son, and that gave me permission to travel on Mobutu's luxurious special presidential boat from Kisangani to Kinshasa.[65] It took about two days to get there.

I stayed with my uncle in Kinshasa. I was very depressed and angry that I could not finish my studies. I took some more exams to keep myself busy, and did some ad hoc teaching in maths and physics at the University of Kinshasa Mont Amba College. My uncle was a pharmacist, and I helped in his pharmacy. He trained me to do prescriptions and medication checks. He also trained me in working in a pharmacy. I went on a couple of business trips to Nigeria for him.

This gave me time to think about getting involved politically. During Mobutu's reign there was only one political party, the MPR (Popular Movement for Revolution). People had to vote, or they would be put in jail: they used to check your fingerprints to see if you had voted. But towards the end he allowed other parties. I joined a pro-Lumumba party, which was led by Mandungu Bula Nyati. There were about 450 parties at that time![66]

Then Kabila[67] came in, leading the Alliance of Democratic Forces for the Liberation of Congo (ADFL), which wasn't a political party. It was a liberation force to kick Mobutu out, a mix of Congolese, Rwandans and Ugandans. Because he didn't have a party, he joined our party and changed the name to GAS (Groupe d'Action pour le Soutien au Président de la Republique). At first I was chosen to go to Belgium, as someone who knew the ideology of GAS, to plan for Kabila's arrival, as he was not liked there, but then they decided to send me to Nigeria, because I had already been there twice. My role was to establish GAS in West Africa. It went well, but it took quite a while because I had to go to court and swear an oath about what I was doing, and to establish sureties and so on

– it was a long process. After that I began to recruit people. I was in Nigeria for almost two years.

While I was there, there was a big demonstration at the US embassy by Congolese refugees in Nigeria. It was organised by Mr Ntonga, who was attaché to the DRC embassy there, and a great friend of Mobutu. He called me to his house and warned me, 'You are very young: don't get involved in this, or you will die very soon.' It was very straightforward. Later on he organised the first attack on Congo from the West, along with Mobutu's wife. They hired a plane, filled it with munitions and flew to Goma, where they picked up trained soldiers and flew them to attack from the West. It didn't work because Kabila started working hand to hand with Angola, and most of those transported from Goma got killed. The ones who came into Kinshasa were just too tired as all food supplies were cut off by Angolan forces: they were captured, scattered across the city, and killed by civilians who put tyres around them and set them on fire.

After the failed coup, Ntonga blamed the demonstration on me. They said that I had a strong connection with America and an American accent. They said I had been working with them, and the Americans had helped me organise the demonstration against Kabila. Finally I was recalled to Kinshasa. Shortly after that, Laurent-Désiré Kabila was killed,[68] and people who were suspected of being against Kabila were accused of plotting.

My first open resistance was coming: I saw kids being recruited for war. People were so fed up with the situation, and couldn't accept it any more. Sometimes there was no electricity for one or two days. Parents were ready to give up their five-year-olds to be trained. There was a recruitment drive for the army, but I was not keen on recruiting kids. You should not recruit anyone under the age of 18; they need to be in education.

I witnessed recruitment at Kamanyola stadium. Before people came, a minister would be on the television, saying, 'We need everyone who is Congolese to come and fight: Rwanda is coming. Even if you don't have a gun, you can use a stick or wire – we need people.' Then they told people to go to the stadium to join up. When I went, there were a lot of lorries lined up on the way in. There were at least six lorries packed with kids leaving Kinshasa for the training camp in Kitona West. They were from about seven years old up; I saw them with my own eyes packed in lorries and leaving.

The next morning there were reports that the lorries were back: they had been ambushed by rebels in Mbanza-Ngungu, and no one knew how many of the kids had been killed. There were so many children who became orphans after the war, and if they got killed no one would know. Kabila had used loads of kids, most of them around 12 or 13, when he took over the country. They wanted me to go back to my own village and recruit from there, but I didn't want to be part of that drive: it was just morally and politically wrong.

That's how I ended up in prison in February 2001. They took me during a meeting and put me in a cell in Makala[69] Prison in Kinshasa. I was there until December, about ten months. I was interrogated quite a few times, by people that I didn't know. At the beginning they beat me: that was normal practice. You could hear other people being beaten in the cells. They promised me that I would be dying 'a slow death'. I came to the point where I wondered if they were going to inject me with poison.[70] I thought, 'Is this the way Lumumba died?' and I got really angry. I remember wishing that all of Congo's wealth would disappear. All the wars we have in Congo are created by wealth: I began to wish that we were like Somalia or the Kalahari Desert. Then no one would be interested in inflicting such pain on us. You realise how small you are, how powerless you are. They move you to a very small cell and keep you there for half a day. You can't work out why they do things, what the pattern is. There was nothing to do, nothing to read. The food was really bad, if you had any, and you just ate to survive. Normally I would never eat kwanga,[71] because it gives me constipation. Sometimes they gave you a piece of dried fish, so then I would eat that and throw the kwanga away.

I never really thought I would get out. The only way I thought I would get out was if I had a gun. And you get to the point where you think you're going mad, becoming a rebel and shooting your way out. None of my family knew I was there. Not even my uncle knew: if he had, he would have informed my family. Even today most of the people in my family don't know what happened. I met my uncle three years ago in Belgium. He came to do some work to do with his pharmacy, and we agreed to meet up.

It was Fred who got me out. I had recruited him for the army when I was in Nigeria, and he had gone up in rank after training in Egypt and was now looking after a regiment. He was doing the rounds in the prison when he saw me. He said, 'What are you doing here? What did you do?'

I said, 'I didn't do anything.' He went away, and I didn't hear any more from him. Then one day they came to get me. I thought it was one of their routines: either I was going to be moved to another place or I was going to be questioned again, or maybe it was someone coming to see if I could give them a connection to get money to pay for my release. But Freddy had arranged everything. I don't know how much he paid. They took me to N'djili Airport and put me on a plane. I didn't know that I was going to the UK; it would not have been my choice anyway. I would have chosen to go to America if I had had a choice. I had connections at the American embassy. Back in 1998 I had won the American Green Card Lottery to go to the States, but I didn't take it up as everything was going fine at that time.

I hadn't had much sleep for a long time, and I was very tired. I had lost a lot of weight too. Now, as a mental health worker, I can see that my mental state back then was a big mess. I was no longer thinking about my family. I had some very destructive thoughts: the kind of powerful force capable of destroying the entire Congo.

The guy who came with me on the plane was from Makala. He never said where we were going; he just put me in his vehicle with two soldiers and drove off until we got to N'djili. From there we flew to Belgium, and then we flew somewhere else – I don't know where. I guess it was an airport near London. To be honest I can't recall the sequence of the trip. After the plane we got on a coach, and it took us to London. We were at a bus station somewhere.

77

When we got there he said he was going back: I didn't believe him at first, because of the length of time it had taken to get there.

I didn't know what to do and didn't know where I was, so I assumed that I had to ask where UNHCR[72] was, but no one knew anything about UNHCR. Eventually someone asked why I wanted it, and told me, 'No, you need the Home Office.' When I was in Nigeria I was told that if a government had good relations with your country, it wasn't a good idea to run there, so I was worried about that.

Someone gave me a ticket to go to the Home Office in Croydon. When I got there it was closed, and it was very cold. I didn't have any warm clothes. I asked someone on the street, and they told me it would be open in the morning. I stayed with someone called Ellie that night, and in the morning there was a queue, so we had to go back again.

At the screening interview in Croydon they assumed, for some reason, that I would not be able to speak English, so they got a French interpreter, who was quite bad. I had to correct him a few times. He was a black guy. I don't know anything about him, except that his French was abysmal and his English was not brilliant either.

From there they put me in a hostel somewhere. I think it was called Portsmouth House. After about a week they put me on a coach with another Congolese guy called Honoré and told us we were going to Manchester. First we were taken to the offices of the accommodation provider,[73] which was PPM, and from there the support worker took us to Parkhouse Street, where we were going to stay. He said that he would come back the following day, which was a Saturday, but he never turned up. The next day, Sunday, was very cold, and we had no heating whatsoever. So my housemate, Honoré, put the electric cooker on full and left it on all the time. We opened the doors upstairs so the heat could get up there.

I remember sobbing: I was still trying to work out why I was there and what might happen. I was still processing everything from the previous months, when I didn't know if I was still going to live. Honoré came in and said he didn't believe in taking drugs but living here would be impossible without taking them, so he decided to start smoking cannabis. He also started going out to try to find people to speak to. He walked all the way to Cheetham Hill[74] and found a Congolese guy on the way, who told him about a Congolese church. I was quite nervous about going there because you didn't know who you would be getting in touch with.[75] We went there – I just wanted to go somewhere to thank God for what had happened – and no one knew us. They only knew that we had come up from London. So we joined the church.

A support worker from PPM finally turned up on the Wednesday, and there was a big confrontation with Honoré, because he thought they had just dumped him there to die in the cold. A year later Honoré decided that he couldn't live like that. He decided that he would rather go and die in Africa than die in England. He put pressure on the Home Office to go back, but they had lost his papers. He went to Refugee Action and they sent him to the Home Office. He went there twice, and both times they told him to go back to the house: they had lost his papers, but they would deal with it. In the end he planned to get a flight to Kenya and claim asylum there. They got him a holding letter and a Kenya Airways ticket. That was his plan. I don't know what happened to him. I never heard from him again.

The Home Office had given me a solicitor from Lewisham, a Nigerian guy. I went there, and he said, 'Don't worry.' I only ever saw my solicitor once. I spoke to him on the phone and asked him what was happening, but he just told me to leave it with him. I had been in Manchester for over a year, and had never had an interview about my case, and never had a letter saying they had refused me either.

Then I had a hearing at a tribunal in Manchester: that was in 2002. The solicitor told me he was going to send a barrister to represent me. When the barrister arrived, he didn't have a clue – he started by asking me where the Congo was and what had happened there! He didn't know anything; he just turned up.

The hearing didn't last very long. The judge asked me a few questions, and that was it. I just remember the shocking thing that the judge said. My house had been burgled and they had taken all my papers, all the documents I had to support my case. The judge asked if I had a police crime number. I gave it to him, and he said, 'This is the way we say, "Welcome to Britain."' I don't know if it was a joke, but in my culture that would be a rude thing to say.

When they burgled the house, they took everything – my medication[76] for the kidney problems I had, my documents, my money, my food. I had nothing to eat. The policeman, PC Warner from Grey Mare Lane, was incredibly supportive. I was being targeted by my neighbours, who kept climbing in at specific times when I was out of the house. I don't know why they did that – just to sell a few things. PC Warner was able to get them evicted.

I went to the Citizens Advice Bureau and they referred me to Mustard Tree.[77] I went to Mustard Tree because I had nothing to eat.[78] I had rung the pastor at my church to tell him about the burglary. I had been going there for a few months, but nobody contacted me or offered me any support – nobody even asked me how I was doing. When I got to Mustard Tree I met Dave Smith. He called Ted, and they said, 'Can we pray for you?' That was what really struck me. I did not know that people I had only just met would feel sad for me, while people I knew just did not care. I think that was what made me draw a line between me and what was seen as the Congolese community. It was a red line really from that point, because I know that it happened to other people, not just me. I can recall a pastor in Bolton telling Honoré that God wanted him to give him all his vouchers (we used to get vouchers to get food from Kwik Save).[79] The pastor used to go and sell them in his shop. That made me angry, and I began to ask 'Why and how does God allow this?'

Mustard Tree gave me a food parcel and ten pounds a week. I used to get that from Pamela, the Zimbabwean lady on reception. After that I started, almost immediately, to volunteer at Mustard Tree. I used to help the Iranian handyman, Javed, with jobs.

A few weeks later I got a letter to say my case had been dismissed, but the solicitor said, 'Don't worry, we can deal with it.' He said he would appeal again, but then he rang to say they had not accepted the appeal. A few weeks later all my support stopped. Thankfully they never threw me out of the house. I stayed there until May 2004.

Then I started to volunteer on the Destitution Project[80] at Mustard Tree. One day when I was volunteering I took a phone call from someone who needed help. When she said her name, I knew it was the neighbour who had been evicted after burgling me. She had moved in with her son. She came in to Mustard Tree, and as soon as she saw me she wanted to run away, but I told her it was alright – I was working for Mustard Tree and helping people in her position. She had come in for a starter pack[81] that we were giving people who had just moved into a house and didn't have anything. I made her a cup of tea and asked her where her son was. She said he ran away when he saw me. I went to look for him and brought him in and sat with them. Then I went to see Mark, the team leader at the time, and asked him if I could give them some of the things that had been offered to me. Then we went to choose a bed from downstairs.[82] They were a bit freaked by me, but I just wanted to let them know that I was there in a different role to support them.

That was my last contact with them before we met in court. It was about two years later when it went to court. I told the police I didn't want to prosecute, but they went ahead anyway because they didn't want them to get off. My neighbour was given 195 hours of Community Service, I think.

I got a new solicitor: Tony, with GMIAU.[83] He said my case had been mishandled. When he contacted the Home Office, they told him that I had to start reporting. Up until then they had not asked me to. Because I didn't have any money for the bus, I used to cycle to Mustard Tree and walk from there to the reporting centre.

I looked online and found out that a church in Wembo-Nyama had been destroyed by rebels, and some old pastors that I knew had been killed. They had also destroyed the hospital. They wrecked the beds and destroyed a generator that provided the power for operations. I had no idea if my parents were OK, and that weighed on my mind a lot. It was a bad time for me, and I was really suffering, but it was quite striking how people at Mustard Tree cared about me. I did not expect people to act in the way they did, like Dave and Bex.

I met Bex at the Destitution Project. She was working for the Red Cross and took over running the project. After a while we fell in love, and in December 2003 we got married and I moved in to her place in Levenshulme. In 2004 Rosie was born, and we moved to Wigan shortly after that. Bex was working, and I was destitute. She was paying for the house and wanted to give me £100 a month, but I wouldn't take it. It's not about pride or anything; it was difficult for me to have someone paying for my house again, so I refused it. At the time I was volunteering at CCP.[84] They paid expenses and for Rosie's childcare: I still have the receipts today! Then, on the day when I wasn't at CCP I would volunteer at the Destitution Project.

There was still nothing happening with my case. By 2006 I had got fed up, and I wrote to the Home Office asking to stay, on the basis that my daughter was a British citizen – under Article 8.[85] They wrote back and said that Rosie could go and live in the Congo with us, that it wasn't dangerous. Our solicitor, who was now Gary McIndoe, appealed against the decision, and we won the appeal because the Home Office failed to turn up twice at the hearing that had been arranged. Then the Home Office appealed *that* decision, and the case was going to go to the high court somewhere in London. It was another year and a half, and still nothing had happened, and I still wasn't allowed to work because they had appealed the decision.[86]

During this time the Home Office had been telling me that they would give me papers if I went back to the Congo and applied to join my wife from there. I got so fed up that I decided to take the risk. We knew someone in Liverpool who was able to arrange my trip. He knew some people in Kinshasa who were in the Presidential Guard, and he paid them to make sure I could get into the country. Bex's father gave us £1,000 to pay for the trip. Then Gary spoke to the Home Office and told them I was going back to the Congo secretly to apply for my visa, and the Home Office told the British embassy in Kinshasa that I would be coming.[87]

So I went. It was a tricky and very risky trip really. The plan was that someone would meet me there. I had already told him what I would be wearing. I flew from Gatwick, and on the plane I met a guy called Scott from Scotland. When we got to Belgium he asked me where I was going, and I told him that I was going to Kinshasa. He said he was going there too. He asked me where I was from, and I told him Manchester. Then he asked me if I supported Manchester United, and I said yes. So we had a chat about

United until we got to Congo. Then he said goodbye, and wished me a safe journey back to Britain. He did not know what I was doing: he just thought I was going there for a few days. He went out first, and my contact picked me up, and I passed through the first three checks without a problem. I got outside in a matter of minutes, where they could not cover me any more. They had arranged for a taxi which was there, but immediately I was surrounded by armed young people. They kept asking questions, in French, like, 'You come from England? You London? You London?'

I replied, 'No, I come from a very small country near the pole called Manchester.'

They were asking lots of questions, when suddenly I saw Scott. He said, 'Maron, what are you doing here?' I could not say anything. At that point I was thinking it was the end, but God had other plans. I was thinking they would kill me, and that maybe I would try to reach and get one of their weapons and discharge it, so they would not live after me. Then Scott came over and held me by the collar and pulled me out. As soon as he did that, two UN vehicles and a British embassy vehicle approached. The soldiers all backed off and started to disappear. He asked them what they were doing there. I could not say or explain anything. I was really too shattered at that point. He pulled me into the British embassy vehicle and put my luggage in too. He asked me where I was going, and I said I didn't know. Then he asked who was supposed to take me, and I showed him the taxi man. He called the taxi man and told him to drive to the place, and we followed him, the taxi in front, then Scott and me in the British embassy vehicle with the two UN vehicles behind us. I did not know until then that he was a European Union military coordinator in DRC.

On the way he really lambasted me. He said it was really too dangerous. There were a lot of checkpoints between the airport and town, and he said we would never have got past the checks. I would have got caught. The taxi took us to a hotel that had already been prepared for me. Scott told me to do what I needed to do next day at the embassy. He offered me his phone to phone Bex, but it was just too stressful at that point. He went back to his car but made a point of coming back and giving me his card, so everyone could see his support for me. He told me, in his very poor French, to call him if I had any trouble, and they would come for me. The owner of the hotel thought I was a CIA guy because I had come with the UN and British embassy vehicles.

There were a lot of young guys with guns downstairs. It was really stressful: I did not sleep all night. In the morning I went out and met Scott. He told me to get out of that place and find somewhere where I would not be seen, and where the people who brought me in would not know where I was.

At the embassy they began to process my visa very quickly because of Gary's communication with them, but they put a wrong date or name on the visa, and then they had a problem with the visa machine for a few days. Then they told me that everything was ready but I would have to pay for a visa for Belgium on the way back. I didn't need one coming to Congo, but they said I needed one going back.

I went to the Belgian embassy, and they told me it would take a week because there was a queue! I said, 'I've got to go back tomorrow,' and that I would never want to go to Belgium. I said, 'It's the last place I want to live in because of the suffering in the Congo which was mainly because of you Belgians!' They spoke to the British embassy and then immediately gave me the passport, even though there was a queue of hundreds in front of me! They just took my passport and told me they would contact me before 12.00. I went back to the British embassy, where I spent a lot of my time during the day.

I phoned the Belgian embassy at one o'clock, and said, 'Listen, you need to do something!' I told them I was going to fly without a visa if they didn't give me one. I went straight to the embassy, and they gave me the visa when I paid. Then I went to the airline, but they said there were no seats left on the flight. I told them I had already paid, and they should get somebody down, because I was ready to die! I had not slept for a long time.

The guy on the desk said, 'OK! OK! You need to get down to the airport now!'

I phoned the agent who was supposed to put me on the flight. He asked where I wanted to meet him, so I said we should meet at the airport. I had gone back to the hotel before coming to the airline and forgot my phone, and when I arrived at the airport, there was no one to meet me. He could not find me. I went and stood at the check-in. I was worried. I had destroyed all my visa paperwork so there was nothing that could be detected.

I saw a guy at the checkpoint talking in my language, Tetela. I approached him and greeted him in Tetela. He asked where I was going, and when I said I was going to England, he said, 'I have friends in England. Can I send them letters?'

I said, 'I don't know where they are. England is so big.' He asked me where I lived, and I said in the North, near Scotland.

So we started talking in Tetela, and he said, 'Can I let you pass?'

I said, 'What do you mean?'

He said, 'This is risky.' Then he took my passport and walked me past the controls to the waiting room without anything being said, and left me there. That was extremely lucky! Before he went back I took all the change out of my pockets, gave it to him, and said, 'Thank you so much!' He didn't know me, apart from the fact that we were both Tetela.

I got on the flight, got to Belgium, and then got another flight to Manchester. That evening Bex had called the guy who should have put me on the plane, and he said he had not seen me. That was a big panic for her. She tried to contact the British embassy, and then she tried to contact Brussels Airline; they told her they could not give her any information. She tried to contact Manchester Airport, and they said they could not give any information about people on the plane. She really got mad and told them I was her husband and that they would have given the information if it had been an American asking! But I got back to Manchester safely.

I got my passport in July 2007, and in September I was offered a job in Kingston upon Thames. Ever since then I have worked, and that has meant I have been able to pay for our housing, which has enabled Bex to do a PHD, which she finished last year. Currently I am a complex needs caseworker working for Elmore Community Services in Oxford. I work with people who have complex mental health issues and can't deal with mainstream services. I work out support plans that will fit their needs and support them at home.

I am desperate to see my parents. It's been far too long. I had no contact from 2001 until 2011, but now I have been in touch. I tried to get information from Wembo through Tom and Kay and they wrote a couple of times, but they were thinking of going to be missionaries in Afghanistan. I lost contact and have no idea where they are now. It was eventually through someone in Canada that I got in touch with my parents. They are OK. I also got more information about Wembo from another friend who lives in North Carolina. One of my uncle's friends emailed me last Christmas to say my parents were thinking of building a villa and they want me to go and live there – but that's not important. I just want to see them really.

When I look back I can see the level of cruelty that is created in the asylum system. I don't know if it was a lack of understanding or an obsession with paperwork. I think of what they put my family through here in Britain. If I could have worked from 2003 to support my wife and daughter, I could have achieved it. I would have had more time for us, more time for me to study, and probably supported more people in a more professional environment. I know I am contributing to society, not to a government, but I think the government is benefiting and getting all the credit.

I know what happened to me, but it's not something I want to dwell on. I am 45 now. The level of stress that was imposed on me, if you look at my head, makes me look like a 60-year-old. I'm not supposed to look like that. It was the sheer level of stress that was imposed on me, not only by Kinshasa but here as well. Unfortunately things like this won't be shown to people who normally deal with these kinds of cases.

On the flip side, I think I am quite lucky to have worked in a mental health environment. I have had a lot of training and understand this stress. Someone who wouldn't understand this would probably have precipitated their life into more chaotic ways of dealing with the stress and traumas. In many places where I have worked, like Mustard Tree and Red Cross, people are supportive and understanding, but in the asylum system it's not like that: they need to come up with a system that understands the background of the people they are dealing with.[88]

I know that I am not a refugee according to the legal definition, just because I have come under a spousal visa, but if I had been accepted as a refugee I would have been free for how many... nine years now? It's not that I don't have money now, but I can't go and see my parents because of the risk and the exposure. I don't want anyone associated with me to be hurt just because I want to visit home.

Even now I am hoping that Kabila goes, and if he does not go in 2016, he's not allowed to stand again according to the constitution, unless he rigs it.[89] But the worry is not Kabila himself – it's his affiliates and those who are close to him. The only hope I have is if he goes, and then the system changes. But it's the whole of Africa ... the way I look at it now, it's just the old system in a different setting. It's not only Kabila; there are so many of those awful dictators being supported by us in Britain. Those psychologically maimed by Charles Taylor[90] are working in Britain to feed him – that's mad!

I also think that Africa has been plundered. What do we in the UK get from Africa? We get all the clever, educated people,[91] and we leave the rest to die there. That's not fair and balanced. I would like to be able to see Africa develop in a different way, keeping their intellectuals and doctors. We go to get doctors from Africa, and what do we give back? Without those doctors, how would the NHS survive? It would crumble within days. At the same time as we do that the media goes on about people coming here to work. Maybe it's time to have an open debate with all this scaremongering going on.

Africa is being emptied in an indiscriminate and sporadic way, not just of natural resources but of intellectual resources. It is a shame, and nobody talks about it. At the same time, we support those people who orchestrate these awful things, like Charles Taylor and Yahya Jammeh[92] and Mobutu.

Africa will never be developed or changed until we learn to avoid past mistakes. Anyone who wants to see Africa develop in a concrete way will not be welcome, because to do that will inconvenience our civilised life here in the West, where we get cheap things from there that benefit us.

I don't really feel angry, but it is just so frustrating, and a shame that that is the way it is.

UK visas – your inflexible friend

There are a hundred things that could be said about Maron's story. There are themes of African dictatorship, corruption, exploitation and postcolonialism. There is disbelief and incompetency in the UK asylum system. There is honesty and morality as Maron spends his years volunteering in a country that has wrongly rejected him. There is so much that is good about British culture, but perhaps the key failing of British society, illustrated through Maron's experience, is its unwavering commitment to *sticking to the rules*, even when that might be counterproductive, or even dangerous.

The Home Office eventually, and grudgingly, admitted that Maron had established a family life here. He had a wife and young daughter, who, having been born here, was also a British citizen. Rather than accept that, as Maron had lived an upstanding life in the UK for many years and was contributing to society, it would be rather good to let him stay here, their first reaction was, 'OK, you have established a family life. Well, you can go and live that family life back in the Congo, then.' Uproot the family. Interrupt the wife's degree and child's schooling: it seemed like they would do anything other than rescind their original, wrong decision to refuse asylum.

When subsequently challenged by a well-respected and determined solicitor, they, again grudgingly, made a further concession: 'OK. We will let him stay here in the UK, but our visa rules say that you have to apply to join your spouse from your country of origin, so we will grant him a visa if he applies for it in the Congo.' The solicitor also challenged this, on the grounds that the normal 60-day wait for a visa would put his life in great danger, so, again reluctantly, they agreed to fast-track the visa.

When they did that, there was an implied admission that indeed, it would be dangerous for Maron to return to Congo – otherwise why not wait the six weeks? And if it was dangerous, then why make him go back there at all? Indeed, why not give him refugee status?

But then, in the UK, *rules are rules.*

---

[58] Patrice Lumumba (1925–1961) was the first democratically elected leader of the newly independent Democratic Republic of Congo. Within 12 weeks of Congolese independence in 1960, Lumumba's government was deposed in a *coup d'état* organised by Colonel Mobutu during the Congo Crisis. Lumumba was subsequently imprisoned and executed by firing squad. The United Nations, which he had asked for help, did not intervene to save him. Belgium, the United States and the United Kingdom have all been suspected of complicity in Lumumba''s death.

[59] The Flemings called Maron *Jim Rice,* after the famous baseball player of the time from the Boston Red Sox.

[60] Mobutu Sese Seko Kuku Ngbendu Wa Za Banga, born Joseph-Desiré Mobutu (1930–1997) was the military dictator and president of the Democratic Republic of the Congo from 1965 to 1997. In 1960, during the Congo Crisis, Belgian forces aided Mobutu in a coup against the nationalist government of Patrice Lumumba. Mobutu then assumed the role of army chief of staff before taking power directly in a second coup in 1965. As part of his programme of 'national authenticity', Mobutu changed the Congo''s name to Zaire in 1971 and his own name to Mobutu Sese Seko in 1972.

Mobutu established a one-party state in which all power was concentrated in his hands. During his reign he amassed a large personal fortune through economic exploitation and corruption (information from https://en.wikipedia.org/wiki/Mobutu_Sese_Seko (accessed 29th March 2016)).

[61] 'The **abacost**, abbreviation for the French *"à bas le costume"* (literally "down with the suit"), was the distinctive wear for men that was promoted by Mobuto as part of his authenticité programme in Zaire, between 1972 and 1990. Zairians were banned from wearing Western-style suits with shirt and tie to symbolise the break with their colonial past. The abacost was a lightweight short-sleeved suit, worn without a tie' (https://en.wikipedia.org/wiki/Abacost (accessed 24th March 2016)).

[62] That day was the anniversary of Mobuto coming to power in 1965.

[63] In 1990, students who had taken part in anti-government protests in Lubumbashi were massacred at night in their university campus. The true story may never be known, as the official death toll was only one, but many believe that Mobuto's miltary butchered hundreds. The blame for the killings was put on the governor of Shaba province, Koyagialo Ngbase, who was sentenced to lifetime imprisonment, but he only served four years of his term. He now maintains that Mobuto made him a scapegoat.

[64] The *Division Speciale Presidentielle* was an elite military force created by Mobutu in 1985 as his personal bodyguard. The soldiers were trained by Israeli advisors and recruited only from Mobutu''s own tribe. The force was used to deal with suspected opponents. People were taken away, tortured, imprisoned without trial, exiled to another part of the country, or simply disappeared.

[65] The River Congo runs from Kisangani all the way to Kinshasa and into the Atlantic Ocean. There are very few ferries, and barges take at least two weeks to cover the 1,000 km.

[66] 'In May 1990, due to … economic problems and domestic unrest, Mobutu agreed to end the ban on other political parties. He appointed a transitional government that would lead to promised elections but he retained substantial powers. Following riots in Kinshasa by unpaid soldiers, Mobutu brought opposition figures into a coalition government but he still connived to retain control of the security services and important ministries. Factional divisions led to the creation of two governments in 1993, one pro and one anti-Mobutu' (https://en.wikipedia.org/wiki/Mobutu_Sese_Seko (accessed 23rd March 2016)).

[67] When the Congo became independent in 1960, Laurent Kabila was deputy commander in the Jeunesses Balubakat, the youth wing of the Patrice Lumumba-aligned General Association of the Baluba People of Katanga (Balubakat). In 1962 he became chief of cabinet for the Minister of Information for North Katanga.

When the Lumumbists formed the Conseil National de Libération, Kabila was sent to eastern Congo to help organise a revolution. In 1967 he founded the People''s Revolutionary Party (PRP) in South Kivu. With the support of China the PRP created a secessionist Marxist state in South Kivu province. This ended in 1988 and Kabila disappeared. Many people assumed that he was dead. However, he was merely making alliances in Rwanda and Uganda.

Kabila returned to Congo in October 1996, leading ethnic Tutsis from South Kivu against Hutu forces, marking the beginning of the First Congo War. With support from Uganda, Rwanda, and Burundi, he led a full-scale rebellion against Mobutu as the Alliance of Democratic Forces for the Liberation of Congo-Zaire (ADFL). He used an estimated 10,000 children in the conflict. By mid-1997, the ADFL had taken over most of the country. Mobutu fled into exile on 16th May and Kabila proclaimed himself president the next day. He suspended the Constitution and changed the name of the country from Zaire back to the Democratic Republic of the Congo.

[68] Kabila was assassinated by one of his bodyguards on 16th January 2001. He was succeeded by his son Joseph eight days later.

[69] Makala Prison is widely renowned as the worst prison in Africa. In 2002, Antoine Vumilia, a political officer in Kabila's regime, was sentenced to life imprisonment for supposed involvement in Kabila''s assassination. He managed to smuggle a camera into the prison, and when he escaped nine years later, dressed as a woman, he told his story to Al Jazeera. You can find his story, and see what he filmed inside Makala, at http://www.aljazeera.com/programmes/witness/2012/05/201252811333 994715.html (accessed 23rd March 2016).

[70] In the Al Jazeeera film there is footage of people being injected.

[71] Chikwanga, or kwanga, made from cassava, is cooked and stored in banana leaves. It is a staple dish, much like rice or potatoes in other countries.

[72] 'The Office of the United Nations High Commissioner for Refugees (UNHCR), also known as the UN Refugee Agency, is a United Nations agency mandated to protect and support refugees at the request of a government or the UN itself' (https://en.wikipedia.org/wiki/United_Nations_High_Commissioner_for_Refugees (accessed 23rd March 2016)).

[73] At the time asylum seeker accommodation was often subcontracted by local authorities to private firms. Standards often left much to be desired, and this particular house was in poor condition. It was also in a poor, predominately white area with a high crime rate.

[74] About five miles away, in North Manchester.

[75] Isolation is a huge issue for asylum seekers. Most do not choose to leave their homeland and culture, so seek every opportunity to connect with compatriots in the UK, especially if they speak little English. However, there is no guarantee that those in your community will share your political or religious allegiance. Indeed, they may even be government spies or from a tribe at war with your own.

[76] The kidney problems only started after coming to the UK. It was sorted by laser treatment. Maron also had an operation to remove the 'foreign body' (a metal splinter) from his arm, which was left over from the beatings in Makala Prison.

[77] See footnote 48.

[78] When Maron came to Mustard Tree, it was very clear that he was in great need. He had not eaten for three days and was in real pain without his medication.

[79] In 2000, despite widespread condemnation from refugee organisations, the then Labour government scrapped the cash-only system for asylum seekers and replaced it with £10 a week in cash and vouchers worth between £18.95 and £26.54 depending on age, which could only be exchanged in local supermarkets.

[80] The Destitution Project started in March 2003. It was set up in partnership with the Red Cross in response to increasing destitution among asylum seekers. Initially they received a food parcel worth around £8, plus £7.50 in cash. As numbers increased each week, the cash element went down to just cover the bus fares to and from the project. By August 2003 more than 80 people were accessing the service every week.

[81] The starter pack consisted of basic cleaning, washing and kitchen items to help people moving into empty accommodation. It was paid for by the Social Services, who had referred the clients to us. Mustard Tree sourced the items from a Cash and Carry as cheaply as they could, and initially didn't even charge the Social Services for time or the fuel, so it was a real bargain for them!

[82] At that time all the donated second-hand furniture was given away free of charge. Gradually, as systems and the quality of goods improved, small charges were introduced for the furniture and delivery. Now Mustard Tree is a growing, thriving charity with several branches serving thousands of disadvantaged people in Greater Manchester (http://www.mustardtree.org.uk).

[83] Greater Manchester Immigration Aid Unit. The solicitor was Tony Openshaw, who went on to set up ASHA (Asylum Support Housing Advice) (https://ashamanchester.wordpress.com (accessed 23rd March 2016)).

[84] The City Centre Project, based in Manchester's Northern Quarter, is now also known as the Young People's Support Foundation.

[85] This refers to a UK law passed in 1998. It means that you can defend your rights in the UK courts and that public organisations (including the Government, the Police and local councils) must treat everyone equally, with fairness, dignity and respect Article 8 of the Human Rights Act is the *Right to respect for private and family life.* It states:

1. Everyone has the right to respect for his private and family life, his home and his correspondence.
2. There shall be no interference by a public authority with the exercise of this right except such as is in accordance with the law and is necessary in a democratic society in the interests of national security, public safety or the economic well-being of the country, for the prevention of disorder or crime, for the protection of health or morals, or for the protection of the rights and freedoms of others.

(https://www.liberty-human-rights.org.uk/human-rights/what-are-human-rights/human-rights-act (accessed 23rd March 2016))

[86] There is something inherently wrong in a system where the Home Office can't be bothered to turn up twice at appeal hearings, then has the gall to appeal the decision taken in their absence. If the asylum seeker missed two hearings they would never be granted asylum in the UK.

[87] Sometimes you have to wonder if rules are more important than human beings in the eyes of the Home Office. Despite the fact that Maron had lived in the UK for six years, and had a British wife and daughter, they still insisted that he should leave the UK, go back to his homeland and apply for a visa from there. Even though they had reluctantly agreed to grant his request and process his application straight away, it seems a totally disproportionate response. Incidentally, if he had not got this 'special dispensation', Maron might well have had to wait for 60 days for the request to be processed, this being the normal length of time it takes to process a spousal visa in DR Congo.

[88] Home Office Asylum Caseworkers are often recruited in their twenties. They have little experience of other cultures, and have to learn fast with minimal training on things like the effect of trauma, yet they are tasked with deciding the fate of people who have fled war, human rights abuses and other forms of persecution.

[89] Most African constitutions only allow a president to serve two terms, yet time and again we have seen dictators change the constitution so they can hang on to power. Mugabe, Museveni, Kabila ... seven African heads of state have so far altered their constitution in order to remain in office.

[90] Charles Taylor was the president of Liberia from 1997 to 2003. He trained as a guerrilla fighter in Libya, and returned to Liberia in 1989 as the head of a Libyan-backed rebel group, the National Patriotic Front of Liberia, to overthrow the Doe regime, initiating the First Liberian Civil War (1989–96). Following Doe's execution, Taylor became one of the most prominent warlords in Africa. He was accused of war crimes and crimes against humanity as a result of his involvement in the Sierra Leone Civil War (1991–2002). In 2003 he resigned, due to international pressure, and went into exile in Nigeria. In 2006 he was extradited back to Liberia. He was tried by the International Criminal Court in The Hague, found guilty in April 2012 of all 11 charges, including terror, murder and rape, and sentenced to 50 years in prison.
(https://en.wikipedia.org/wiki/Charles_Taylor_(Liberian_politician) (accessed 29th March 2016))

[91] David Cameron often says that he wants the 'brightest and best' people to come to the UK. In March 2013 he said in a major speech,

'Now, that means ensuring that those who do come here are the brightest and the best, the people we really need, with the skills and entrepreneurial talent to help create the British jobs and growth that will help us to win in the global race.' If we 'win' in the global race, by taking everybody else's 'brightest and best', then surely the countries that have trained them, at their own expense, are the losers – even if they are developing countries? A good example is the recruitment of nurses from Africa. It is easy to persuade nurses trained in countries like Ghana and Malawi, where pay is low and conditions often difficult, to come to the UK for salaries that can be 20 times higher. The effect, however, is to leave African hospitals seriously understaffed, and the nearest nurse a day's journey for many rural Africans, as CNN reported in 2003,
http://edition.cnn.com/2004/WORLD/africa/08/03/nurses.uk/index.html?eref=sitesearch (accessed 23rd March 2016).

[92] Yahya Jammeh is the president of the Gambia. He took power in a 1994 military coup. He was elected as President in 1996; he was re-elected in 2001, 2006 and 2011, in what were commonly held to be fraudulent elections. An absolute dictator, he has declared Gambia an Islamic Republic, vowed to execute every gay and lesbian in Gambia, and suppressed media freedom, as well as introducing bizarre herbal treatments that he claims can cure HIV, asthma and infertility.

Mary's story

I was born in the city of Abadan, in the province of Khuzestan in south-west Iran in 1955. Abadan is right on the border with Iraq. It's a very important oil city. It was built like British cities when they built the huge oil refinery there. The buildings are just like they are in England, with gardens.

I am the fourth of five children. My father was a senior official in the oil company – a very important man and a real gentleman. I was a happy child. I grew up when the Shah was in power, before the revolution.

Because Abadan is very near to Kuwait, lots of Arabs used to come there. I had left high school and was working in a Middle Eastern bank. Then I met a gold merchant from Kuwait, and fell in love. I was 18 when we married. He was 35. I was very happy and went to live with him in Kuwait. When I got there I found out that he had two children living with him from a previous marriage. He hadn't told me about that, and he wasn't honest with me, but I didn't mind, because I was very young, and they were two lovely boys. So I started my married life with two children!

After that I returned home to Iran to tell my parents, but I was happy with the situation because my husband was a very good man: he was respectful and easy-going. He was also very rich.

While I was living in Kuwait, the revolution happened in Iran, and Ayottolah Khomeini[93] came to power. It was just after the big fire in the Cinema Rex,[94] which killed hundreds of people. There were lots of anti-Shah demonstrations on the streets, and people everywhere. There were also a lot of government soldiers about. My mother was on her way to visit her sister when she was shot dead by soldiers – or maybe by Khomeini's men; we are not sure, because Khomeini's people often made trouble. It was an automatic rifle that killed her. She was hit in several places. I was coming back from Kuwait for a visit, and when I arrived I didn't see my mum. They told me what had happened a week later.

When I returned to Kuwait, the situation got worse. There were lots of demonstrations, and many people were shot. They closed the airports, stopped the ferries and cut off the phones: Iran was cut off from neighbouring countries, including Kuwait. I was very upset because I had no contact with my family. I cried and cried.

Then one day, just 40 days after my mother died, my husband came in wearing a black shirt. I asked him what had happened, but he said it was nothing. Then my brother-in-law came and told me that my father had died too. I could not stop crying, and felt I had to go back home to my family, but there was no way I could get back. As a woman I couldn't go alone, because women don't go out on their own in Kuwait. It was very difficult to be a woman in that society, but I agreed to wear the hijab[95] because I loved my husband.

My brother-in-law was a very powerful man in the country, and he said he would arrange for me to go home through Iraq in his car with a chauffeur. It's only four or five hours' drive. My mother-in-law, who was a lovely woman, agreed to come with me.

At the Iraqi border the soldiers ordered me to take off my face covering. My mother-in-law told them that my husband didn't allow that, but they said that I could not enter the country unless I showed my face. When I took off the covering the soldiers made some rude noises, but they let us through, and we made it back to my parents' house. When we arrived, I discovered that my father had actually died from a heart attack when visiting my mother's grave in the cemetery. He never got over my mother's death, and died of a broken heart. My mother was 45 when she died, and my father was in his early fifties. My father was buried next to my mother.

After about a month I returned home to Kuwait with my mother-in-law. All the airports and roads were closed, so this time we had to go by boat. It was a big fishing boat, but not safe with 25 people on board. It took about a day.

My life went on, but I was very sad, and I asked my husband if I could go and live back in my own country. Before, I was happy to live in Kuwait, because I still had my parents back home and I could go and visit them, but now they were dead I missed my family and my country so much. My husband agreed and bought me a big house in a very posh area in Khorramshahr near Abadan. His two children came with me, because they really needed me. They were about three and four years old.

Within a year of coming back, before the children had started school, the war started between Iran and Iraq.[96] Khorramshahr[97] is right on the Iraqi border, just across from Basra. It's only a few miles away. My husband came and took all the valuable things back to Kuwait – we had a lot of gold – and then he took us in the car, along with my sisters and brother, to another city, Shiraz, which was further away from the fighting.

After a year my husband wanted to go back to Kuwait, but I couldn't leave my family while the war was going on, and the children didn't want to leave me, because I had become their mum. I had also become pregnant by then, and gave birth to a daughter. After my daughter was born, I began to feel happier, and although the war was still going on, it wasn't as bad as before. My husband was coming backwards and forwards between Kuwait and Iran, and I soon became pregnant again. This time the baby was a boy.

Then my husband decided to move us again, this time to a big house in Shemiran, a very posh area in the north of Tehran. My brother-in-law and his wife came too. I didn't forget about the deaths of my mother and father, but I was coping well, and looking after the four children. My husband travelled regularly from Kuwait, and I also returned there for a short while. It was while I was there in Kuwait City that the Iraqis suddenly attacked Kuwait.[98] Everything happened so fast – rockets and explosions everywhere. The Iraqis looted the big shops, stole gold and set fire to lots of places.

We got out quickly back to Iran, leaving my husband's assets behind. He left us there and returned to Kuwait, because he was worried about his business. Then one night, he went to sleep and never woke up. He had died in his sleep.

For me, too many bad things had happened. First my mum, then my dad, and now my husband...

I was thinking that life could go on, because I had my babies, my children, but all the money had now finished. I had the big house and expensive gold jewellery, but the income was gone. I said to myself, 'OK. Life must go on. I will bring up my children, look after them, study accountancy and work to support my children.' I got my diploma in accountancy. My mother–in-law was so helpful. While I was studying she looked after the children: she was just like a mother to me. If she had not been so supportive, I don't know what I would have done.

I passed my exams and was able to work as an accountant in various places. This went on for a long time, until my sons were very big. All the time I had no boyfriend. If I had married again, I would have had to leave the children with my in-laws,[99] because that's the way things are in Arab countries. So I didn't think about men, just about my children.

After about ten years the older boys decided to get married. They were about 27 or 28 years old by then. The boys did not have any of their father's money, but they needed dowry money in order to get married. So, with the agreement of my mother-in-law, I sold the house and we rented a smaller house. It was shortly after that, before the second son married, that my mother-in-law died. She was 87 years old but had been very active, not like an old woman.

So now there was just me, along with my own daughter and son who lived with me. One weekend we decided to go to the seaside near Chalus, north of Tehran, for a break. I went with my son while my daughter, who was engaged, stayed behind in Tehran. While we were there we met a very nice man called Mohamed. He said to my son, if we needed anything, we could call him, as he had a nice villa nearby. He had my son's number, and he called him. He asked me if I wanted to meet him. I told him that I had not been in a relationship for a long time. I said I couldn't have a relationship until my children had left home.

It isn't allowed for people to live together without being married in Iran. You have to be married. But there is something called 'temporary marriage'[100] in Islam. It's not like a complete marriage, but it's not like being unmarried either. So we agreed to have a temporary marriage for one year. During that time my daughter and son both got married, so then I was free to marry permanently.

During the temporary marriage my husband was very good, but I never knew what Mohamed did for a living. I just knew he was in business. He told me that he was in a private company. He had a big Islamic beard and moustache, but he was a real gentleman, helping my son to find a good job as an engineer, helping my daughter with her marriage. He would come for a coffee while I cooked, and then he would leave. If we went out, he treated me very well, opening the car door for me, not like many Muslim men in Iran, who walk in front of their wives and order them around. So when my children were married, I decided I would like to marry him permanently. I was 53 years old, and he was nearly 60.

About a week after we were married, Mohamed changed completely. He started to order me around like a dictator. One day I came back from shopping, and he started to shout and hit me. 'Who let you go shopping without me?' he yelled.

'But I have been doing that all the time,' I said. I told him I would not go out without him, but that didn't stop him being violent. He often hit me without any reason at all. I just had to stay at home and do the cooking. I even had to change my work. Before that I had gone to different companies for a few hours each time to do my accounting, but now I said I would bring the work back home and work from there – but he would not allow me to work at all, either outside or at home.

Sometimes he would say he was going away to another city on business, but he never told me where he was going, so I don't know if he was telling the truth. I like to spend time with my relatives, and I was feeling very sad, so one day when he was away I went to my sister's house. My husband came and took me back home.

Next door to my sister lived a man and his sister. I met her a few times, and we chatted together. She told the man about my situation. One day I went over to their house and met the brother. His name was Karim. We chatted together. We talked about our lives. I told him about my difficult situation, and I began to feel that I liked this man. He was a few years younger than me. I don't know why I let it happen – maybe because I had been on my own for so long or maybe it was because of my age, and my feelings were changing... I don't know why I did it. I had a husband, and I wasn't supposed to speak to another man, but I didn't care, because he had abused me so much. I had never done anything like this before, but I just wanted to run away from my husband and be with this man. I felt so lonely and stressed. Sometimes his sister would go out, and we were left together. We were too close.

One day Karim came to my house. I knew that Mohamed could shoot me if he found out, but I didn't care. And he did find out. He came back one night and caught us together. I nearly died with fright. Karim opened the door and let me get out, and I ran to my nephew's house nearby, leaving them in the house together. That was the last time I saw Karim. I never found out what happened to him. It was about eight o'clock at night. My nephew was scared that the neighbours would find out and talk, so my nephew and niece drove me straight away up to Chalus, where I would be safe. I had nothing with me, not even a change of clothes.

My husband had been so bad, such a dictator, and had abused me both verbally and physically, that I had already taken my documents, my gold and some clothes to my sister's house. I knew that he would kill me now if he found me, and Chalus was only two or three hours' drive from Tehran.

Early the following morning my sister rang my niece to tell her that Mohamed had been to her house with the police, looking for me. They had brought a video with them and showed it to them. I had no idea that my husband had put a camera in our house, and the film showed us having an affair. My sister was angry that I had done that, and said that she was no longer my sister.

I knew that there was no way I could stay in the country. I would have been killed, either by the government or by my husband, or even my family. If you have a relationship with another man when you are married, you will be killed.[101] If my son had seen that film, even seen me speaking with another man, maybe it would have been better to be dead. I had to get out.

My niece and her husband drove me to a village near Urmia not far from the Turkish border. I didn't have any money to help me escape, so he paid a man to get me into Europe through Turkey. We only stayed there one night in a cottage. Two men came that night and asked my niece's husband for the money: he paid them around five million toman.[102] That was a deposit; he was also going to get the same amount again at the end of the journey, when I was safe.

The next morning a man came very early, at about three or four o'clock. I said goodbye, and we set off. I didn't know where we were going. He drove for a while without lights up into the mountains; then we got out and walked for three or four hours down the other side until we came to a lorry. I don't know, but I think we must have crossed the border into Turkey. The man spoke to the driver in Turkish and paid him some money. The driver told me to get in the lorry and keep quiet. He said I should hide in a corner behind all the boxes in the back of the lorry. He gave me a duvet and blanket to sit on, and told me to wear my coat, because it was black and I wouldn't be seen.

The car driver said goodbye and left. For the first time I felt that I was safe, because I was finally outside my country. I don't know how long we had been travelling, because I fell asleep, and when I woke up it was dark. We went on for another four or five hours, and then the lorry stopped. Another man opened the door and gave me a small box of food. He asked if I needed the toilet, but I said no: I was scared, because I was alone with two men. I only ate the biscuits and bread and drank the water, which was in a sealed bottle, because I didn't know what was in the other food – I didn't trust the men, and was afraid it might be unsafe or poisoned.

I got very hungry because I wasn't eating much for several days. The driver told me that we would only stop after it had got dark. Then I could get out and go to the toilet and wash. This went on for five or six days. During that time I had no idea where I was, or which country we were in, because it was always dark. Twice we changed lorries, each time after one and a half or two days. The second time, when I got in I found there was a couple already in the lorry. I don't know where they were from. They weren't Iranian or Turkish: I didn't understand their language and they didn't speak English. I think maybe they were from Greece or Cyprus or something. They were very scared.

After a while the engine stopped, but I still didn't know where we were. I was really frightened. I could still hear some noise; I think we must have been on a train or a ferry – I don't know which. The driver had told us not to move and to be quiet until he knocked on the door and let us out. A few hours later the engine started up, and we were moving again.

Finally the lorry stopped, and the driver opened the door. He said, 'Go, go, go!' and shoved us out. We were somewhere near Manchester. The couple ran off, but I was caught by the police. They took me to the police station and asked me questions, but I didn't understand – but I knew 'yes', 'no', 'Iranian' and 'asylum' in English, and kept saying that.

They sent me to Refugee Action in Manchester. I was very dirty from being in the back of the lorry, so they gave me a towel and told me to take a shower. I was also very hungry, because I had only eaten biscuits and a few bits of sandwich for a whole week.

Refugee Action gave me food, and bed and breakfast in a hotel in the city centre because there were no spaces on the coach to London that night. The next morning someone from Refugee Action came and took me to the coach station and put me on a coach to London.

On 8th September 2010 I went to the Home Office in Croydon: I had arrived in the country on 6th September. I explained my situation – that I was from Iran, and what had happened with my husband. They wrote it down and sent me to a hostel in London for one night, and the next day someone from the Home Office came. Some were sent to the North, and some to the South. I was sent to Birmingham.

At this time I was just thinking about all the things that had happened to me. I was in a hostel in Birmingham, and after a week I went to see a solicitor to get legal aid. I didn't speak very good English, so they gave me an interpreter, but he was from Afghanistan. Farsi and Dari are the same language, but not completely the same – sometimes there are differences. I told them about my life, about everything that had happened to me, and why I had come to England.

Mary's Journey

Stage 1 : Iran and Kuwait

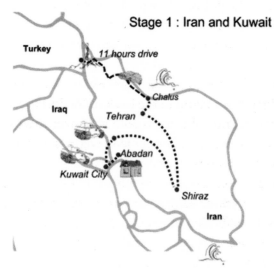

Stage 2: Europe

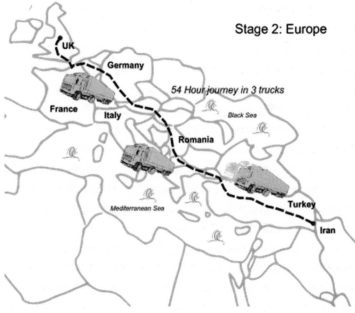

After about a week I was sent for the Home Office interview. It lasted about two hours. I had a good interpreter this time, a proper Farsi speaker.

About two weeks later they moved me to another hostel in Birmingham. I arrived there on the Saturday, and the next day I went to church. When I lived back in Iran I was Muslim. I had a friend who was a Christian – Armenian Orthodox. Sometimes we would chat together over coffee, and she would talk about her religion. After what my husband did to me, I came to hate his Islamic religion. I believed that God was everywhere, so I started to go to the Iranian church in Birmingham every Sunday to pray.

Then I received a refusal letter from the Home Office. I was very sad, but people told me it was normal to get a refusal at first. My solicitor put in an appeal. The Home Office believed what I said about the problem with my second husband, but didn't believe the reason why I did not marry from 28 until I was in my fifties. They didn't understand that I was not allowed to marry again and keep the children of my first husband. They didn't know about my culture, and did not accept what I said.[103]

The solicitor put in an appeal. This time I had to go to a court in Birmingham and answer questions from the judge. It was over very quickly. It lasted less than half an hour. I was just asked two questions by the judge. Two months later, in March 2011, it was refused again. I didn't understand why it was refused.

I was now going to a church which was not just for Iranians. I remember one lady, who was also called Mary. I was in a meeting for new Christians in her house.

Then my support was stopped: I had no money, no accommodation, no family, and I didn't speak much English. I just had an Iranian friend called Azita* living in Manchester. She was actually my sister's friend. When my big sister found out that I was having an affair, she had disowned me. She said, 'I never had a sister!' My brother and the rest of my family, even my son and daughter, said the same. I found all this out after I had been refused. When I escaped, I did not have any phone numbers with me. They were just in my memory. And when I was able to speak to my niece, that's what she told me.

I was so depressed, I decided to kill myself. I went to the big roundabout at Five Ways in Birmingham. I was going to close my eyes and run into the road. But an Iranian friend knew about my situation, and knew I was suicidal. She spoke to a lady who supported Asian women. This lady talked to me about what she could offer. She used an Iranian with good English to interpret for her. She told me not to worry, and said she would help with advice.

At the same time I met a gay Iranian called Reza* who had been granted asylum very quickly. It's really dangerous to be gay in Iran. It isn't allowed at all. He offered to let me stay with him in his hostel in Stoke-on-Trent. There was also an Iranian and his wife living in Wolverhampton, who said the same. I spent a day or two with Reza and about a week with the family in Wolverhampton.

Then I was able to get in touch with Azita, my sister's friend. She had come to the UK to study when she was young. She had got married here, and was living in a big house in the Didsbury area of Manchester with her daughter, after getting divorced from her husband. My niece gave me her number, so I called her. I told her my situation, and she told me to come to Manchester to stay with her. I will never forget Reza, the guy from Stoke. He is a good human being. He gave me money for the bus fare to get to Manchester. We are still in contact today.

Azita met me at the coach station. The first week we spoke a lot about my sister and family and everything going on in Iran. Then Azita told me I could stay if I did some work in the house. I started going to a Catholic church near her house: I had come to believe in Jesus. A few months later I got baptised in church. I felt that someone was looking after me, and it made me feel so much better.

In August 2011 Azita went to Iran to visit family. While she was there she collected all of my documents and brought them back together in one packet, including my passport, driving licence and ID, as well as documents from the oil company and my gold. She also spent some time with my sister and told her about my life here. My sister became a little softer towards me, but not completely. When Azita came back, she brought £100 from my sister, brother and niece for my birthday on 22nd September. I was so pleased to hear that my family still accepted me as one of the family. It really helped to know that.

When Azita returned, she told me that she had a lump in her breast. I went with her to Nightingale Hospital to be checked. A few days later she heard that she had breast cancer. She cried and cried. She was a very rich lady, and had kept the house and a flat as well after the divorce. Her ex-husband owned a takeaway.

She started coming with me to church every Sunday after that. She had an operation, and after the chemotherapy her hair began to fall out. Every night I would wake up hearing her crying loudly. I was looking after her, and also doing all the work in the house: shopping, washing, cleaning and cooking. I showered Azita and took her to hospital, and didn't get any money for doing it, just my room and food.

At this point I decided to make a fresh claim because I was now a Christian. I couldn't go back to Iran. I got legal aid from South Manchester Law Centre, and started to put together my case. It was the Christmas holidays: the Law Centre was closed, so I couldn't take my evidence.

Then on 5th January 2012 everything changed. It was very early in the morning, round about six o'clock, and I was asleep in my bed when I heard a knock on the bedroom door. I wrapped the blanket round me because the house was so cold. It was very expensive to heat in the winter. Then I saw two men in uniform. They said, 'Come on, get up!'

I thought, 'Oh God, Azita has died!' I said, 'Can I get my dressing gown?'

They said, 'No! Don't touch anything!' I came downstairs, and there were two more men there in uniform. Then I saw Azita in the living room.

I said, 'Thank God!' and asked her in Farsi, 'Who are these men?'

'Immigration,' she replied.

I asked them why they were here, and they said I was here illegally. I told them about the fresh claim, but they still said I was illegal. Then I saw there were even more –

eight in total: three women and five men. They had a van outside with a grille in it, like for criminals. First they told Azita she was not allowed to talk to me; then they got an interpreter on the phone. He told me they were taking me to detention, and I would be taken back to Iran. I said, 'OK. I believe in God and in Jesus. If it happens, it happens.' All the same, I was very scared.[104]

They took me to Manchester Airport, still in my pyjamas. They did not allow me to get changed, or even to go to the toilet. I said to them, 'OK, I am illegal here, but I am not a criminal – I am a human.' When I got to the airport and saw the planes, I thought they were going to put me straight on a plane back to Iran. If that happened, I knew I would not even go before a judge – they would just kill me when I got back to Iran.

They kept me there at the airport, still in my pyjamas, for two days. I was given food and a bed, but I had no other clothes except a coat with me. Then they gave me a card with the name 'Yarl's Wood' on it. That's where they were taking me, to the women's detention centre.

When I got there it was just like being a real criminal. They did a full body search, and I could always hear the noise of gates and doors being locked. It was just like a prison. I decided that if I could find anything to kill myself with, I would do it. It wasn't that I was worried about myself: I was worried about my children. My culture would not accept what I had done, and I believed that my children would be in danger because of me.

They gave me some new clothes when I got there. The shoes they gave me were too big. I take a size five, and they gave me size six or seven. The clothes were also too big. I was a size 12, and they gave me size 16.

I didn't understand about mealtimes either. The women with children had to go on one side, and the rest the other side. I still did not speak English very well, because I always spoke Farsi to Azita. I was always in the house and was not allowed to go to college, so I never spoke much English.

I found another Iranian in the centre and borrowed her phone to call Azita. I asked her to find a solicitor for me, and to use the gold that I had to pay for it, because the lady had told me that I would need a private solicitor to get me out of Yarl's Wood. Azita found me a solicitor at Latitude Law, and I told him that I had some new evidence for a fresh claim. He said he would get the documents from my room and start to prepare the claim.

This Iranian lady also came to church there to pray. I would ask her things there. I told her that I wasn't well. I had palpitations and the shakes, and had begun to lose a lot of weight. I think it was stress. I went to the GP and told him about it, but he told me to go away and take paracetamol.[105] I told him I wasn't in any pain, but he didn't listen. He told me he didn't care and to go away. In one month I lost ten kilos. I rang my solicitor, and he managed to get me out and get me an appointment with a doctor back in Manchester.

I came back to Azita's house and went to the GP next day. He told me that I had an overactive thyroid, and that I had come to him too late – I should have come to him before. I told him I couldn't because I was in detention. They sent me straight to Wythenshawe Hospital. They found that I had an infection, and sent me to Christie's Hospital. There they did some more tests. My eye had started to pop out because of the thyroid. At Christie's they tried different drugs on me, because they said that it was too late. I felt that I was being experimented on like a mouse in a laboratory! Every day they gave me steroid injections, but it wasn't good. Then I had radiotherapy; my eyes were really bad, and I cried a lot. I also went to church a lot to pray.

The hospital changed my medication and the dosage all the time, and when I eventually felt well enough, they did a quick operation to take out the thyroid. They told me that they had to do that, because if they didn't I would lose my sight in that eye.[106]

In January 2013 Edward put in the fresh claim on the basis of my faith, and I was given asylum support[107] again, accommodation in Northenden and some cash. I shared a house with a Zimbabwean lady called Mavis, who became a very good friend. She told me about places for asylum seekers where I could go, like WAST[108] and City of Sanctuary.[109]

When it came to the court hearing, the Father from my church came with me to testify that I am a real Christian, but the judge said that he didn't believe that I was. My solicitor said that the priest was the expert in religion,[110] not the judge, but I was still refused, and my asylum support finished then too. I had just been in my accommodation for two months.

Again I had no money. My gold had all been sold to pay £5,000 for the solicitor fees. I had nothing left. Mavis told me to go to the Red Cross Destitution Project, where I could get a food parcel and five pounds a week. I moved back in with Azita, but this time I couldn't do all the housework because I was ill. After a while Azita told me that I couldn't stay any longer, because her daughter needed the room.

I talked to other Iranians at the Red Cross and WAST, and they advised me what to do. I spent some nights with other Iranians, some nights with an English family that I had met through a church minister at the Red Cross, and some nights at Azita's. But it was difficult for me to move around from place to place, because my radiotherapy meant it was dangerous to be near babies or pregnant women. I also have sickle-cell anaemia. When I had a reaction to my medication, my whole body was covered in a black rash. I still have some on my body.

Then, when I had been going to the Red Cross for nearly a year, they told me that my support there would be stopping, because they could only support for one year. At that point they told me about the Boaz Trust – round about November or December 2013. So I came to Boaz and met Bénédicte, and told her my story. She wrote everything down, but told me there were a lot of people waiting for a place in the houses, so I would have to wait. I remember one day going to Azita's and she told me I couldn't stay that night, so I spent hours just walking around and wondering why it was happening to me. I slept in Fog Lane Park and woke up really cold. Then I went back to Azita's house.

I had to wait a long time until there was a place for me in a Boaz house. I rang Bénédicte every day, but the answer was always, 'I'm sorry, we don't have a space yet.' Then, on 28th March 2014, as I was walking along the street,

Bénédicte called me and asked me if I could come to Boaz. When I got there she told me that Boaz had found accommodation for me. I was so happy, and was thanking God all the time. She said, 'You can go there tomorrow.'

I said, 'Can't I go today?' I was worried that someone else would get the place before me, but she told me not to worry.

I came the next day with just a small suitcase. I imagined all sorts of things about the house – maybe that it would be overcrowded, or that it wouldn't be clean, because it was for homeless people. She took me on the bus to the house in Old Trafford.

When we got there I was amazed how big and how nice the house was, but I told Bénédicte that I couldn't go upstairs easily because of the problem with my eyes. She showed me a big room downstairs with a wardrobe. I was so thankful to have a roof over my head, and to feel safe. I was also very happy that there was another Iranian lady, Susan, living in the house. I told all my friends about the big house I was living in. It was such a good feeling.

This was the beginning of the next step in my life. I started to join in lots of activities at places like WAST. I joined the choir there, began art classes, and started to attend English classes at Boaz, where I could learn how to read and write in English. For the first time I felt settled, so I could do these things.

Bénédicte told me that Boaz could help with other support, and I asked if she could find me a solicitor, as I had not had one for a long time. She spoke to Raj, the Boaz solicitor, and I had an appointment about a month later. I had a few documents, but most of them were still with the private solicitor. At first they wanted £100 before they would send them over, but in the end they let Raj have them for free when he said he would get them from the Home Office instead.

At the interview I had a Farsi interpreter. Raj asked me if I was going to church: I told him that I was going every week to the Catholic church on Palentine Road, and that I had been baptised there. He said that he would put in a fresh claim for me if I could get some evidence of that.

That summer I had two operations on my eyes, and my health improved a lot, but I was still worried about my asylum situation. I used to get scared every time I had to report to Dallas Court. I had to go every month, and I could never sleep before reporting.[111] I was always thinking of what might happen if I was detained again and sent back. I was 100 per cent sure that I would never get out of the airport alive. They would kill me there. I would never even see a judge. So when I went to Boaz to get my bus ticket I would be shaking in fear.

This made me start to act like I had Alzheimer's: I kept forgetting things. Once I even put my glasses in the fridge! On one occasion I had an appointment at Christie's Hospital, but instead I got the bus to my GP by mistake. It was only when the receptionist asked me if I had an appointment that I realised I was in the wrong place!

One day I was in my church praying. I always took all my valuables with me, because at the time I didn't have a lock on my bedroom door. When I entered the church, there was no one except an old man sitting there in the corner. I put my bag down on the chair and went forward to pray and light a candle. I was there for 10 or 15 minutes thanking God for my accommodation and everything else. When I came back my bag was gone, and no one was there to see what had happened. It had my house keys, phone, bus pass, Home Office documents, ID card and money in it.

I went to see Father Kelly. He told me not to worry because there was a CCTV camera. He called the police, and they came and took a statement. Then I went to Azita's house. I was crying and asking God, 'Why did this happen?'

Azita took me back to the Boaz office. I gave Katie[112] the police letter. She was wonderful. She told me not to worry, arranged for a new key, phoned the Home Office to get a new ID and called my doctor for some new tablets. I didn't feel any more that it was a problem that I had lost my phone and bag – I could buy new ones. I felt good again, because I was still here, and Boaz was here for me too. I could relax and continue with my activities as normal.

When the police looked at the CCTV film, they saw a man come from the back of the church, look around and take my bag. He quickly left the church, but as he went outside he ran into a baptism party. They were taking family photos, and when the thief went past, he was caught in the photo too! I have now got that photo of the family together with the thief! The police told me later that the thief and his two brothers were always stealing things. It was his second crime that week. But I never did get my possessions back.

One day in May 2015 Katie rang me to say that my fresh claim was ready. I had new evidence from my doctor and from my daughter – everything was complete. I had to take it to Liverpool in person. I got the train there and handed my documents in. It took just a few minutes for them to check the fresh claim; then they told me I could go.

Normally you get Section 4 accommodation if they accept your fresh claim. That means that you will be given accommodation somewhere and get an Azure Card[113] instead of money. I was afraid that I might be sent somewhere a long way from Manchester. I was thinking about that all the time.

One day – it was 19th June – I came home to find a card saying that I had to collect a letter from the post office which needed signing for. The next day I went to the post office and collected a big packet. I thought it was about the Section 4 accommodation. I was wondering what was in it, thinking where I might be sent and worrying that it would not be as good as the Boaz house.

I didn't open the packet there. Instead I caught the bus and came straight to Boaz. I told Katie about the packet, and told her I thought it was about the Section 4 house. She asked if she could open it, and I said yes – *I* didn't want to. She read it, and said, 'You've been granted leave to remain!'

I can't forget the feeling I had at that moment. I was so happy. I was crying and shaking and thanking God – I couldn't believe it! I was so excited: I couldn't control my emotions! I went to church to give thanks and also to say sorry to God for being mad about my bag! I also went to see Vicki at WAST to tell her my news. WAST has been so important as a place to meet with other women asylum seekers to share things together, and to take part in drama, the choir and other things. After that I came back to Boaz to share my happiness with my Boaz family. Katie is like a daughter to me: when I met her parents I said to them, 'Take care of my daughter! I am her second mum!'

Sometimes when I wake up in the night, I wonder whether it is all real, or whether I have dreamt it all! Then I look at the letter and realise that it's genuine; then I can go back to sleep again. When I come to Boaz on the bus, I am always thinking about what will happen next, but Katie has helped me with the National Insurance number and the Job Centre, and things like that. I am so thankful to my God for everything I have – for my health and for my freedom. I am no longer scared of being sent back home. I can now speak to my son, my daughter and my grandson. Although I can never return to Iran, my family can come over to Europe and I can meet them there. My relationship with my sister is much better now too. At first it was very hard to speak to her at all, but when I was ill she began to soften. Now things are much better between us.

One of the first things I did after I got my papers was to go home and put all the clothes, even my shoes, that I used to wear to go to Dallas Court into a bin bag; then I gave them all away to charity. I never want to remember them again! Sometimes it used to be raining or snowing at Dallas Court, but we used to have to stand outside and wait, because they didn't let us in until it was our turn.

You know, since I got my papers, everything around me seems like it's a different colour. Everything looks different to me: it's bright, not dark. The trees are beautiful, the garden is beautiful – even the street looks beautiful!

I want to stay in Manchester. I want to go to college and learn English properly, not just English for chatting, and when my English is better I want to get a job. At the moment I am volunteering at Mustard Tree. I have my food hygiene certificate, and last week I made the food for a City of Sanctuary meeting.

In the long term I want to help and support asylum seekers like Boaz does. I can work voluntarily or support them in church. I don't have that much time left – I will be 61 this September, and I want to use that time to help other people. I was once destitute with no money or home, and I want to help others that are in the same situation now. Sometimes, when I look back, I can see how God has helped me. When I had such hard problems, God helped me.

I have changed inside. My thinking has changed too, and I have hope for the future. Inside I am happy, happy, happy. Thank God. I just want to help others and enjoy life with friends.

A changed life

If anyone has a reason to moan about life, Mary has. She was caught up in two wars. Her mother was murdered, her father died of a broken heart and her husband dropped dead one night at a young age. She lost her homes and all her wealth, was tricked into marriage with a man who turned out to be repressive and violent, and had to flee her country.

Having escaped one hell, she found herself in another. Refused asylum, destitute in a foreign land, caring for a lady with cancer, demeaned and degraded in detention, facing the possibility of being sent back to her death, and with serious medical problems – what more could possibly have gone wrong in one person's life?

Yet, if you meet Mary you will find a lady who has no bitterness, and who is full of hope for the future. What can be the reason for that? As she says herself, 'When I had such hard problems, God helped me.' Mary's story is a testimony to the life-changing grace of God that is found in Jesus Christ.

---

[93] Ayatollah Khomeini (1902–1989), was an Iranian Shia Muslim religious leader, politician, founder of the Islamic Republic of Iran and the leader of the 1979 Iranian Revolution which deposed the Shah of Iran. Following the revolution, Khomeini became the country's Supreme Leader, a position which he held until his death.
[94] On 19th August 1978 the Cinema Rex in Abadan, Iran, was set ablaze, killing at least 470 people. It started when men barred the doors and doused the place with petrol before setting it alight. Although a Captain Tahiri was found guilty as the perpetrator, and consequently executed, his guilt is widely disputed, and after a later trial five Islamic militants were found guilty and executed.
[95] 'A hijab ... is a veil that covers the head and chest, which is particularly worn by some Muslim women beyond the age of puberty in the presence of adult males outside of their immediate family.' (https://en.wikipedia.org/wiki/Hijab (accessed 24th March 2016))
[96] The Iran–Iraq War lasted from September 1980 to August 1988. It began when Iraq invaded Iran on 22nd September.
'It followed a long history of border disputes, and was motivated by fears that the Iranian Revolution in 1979 would inspire insurgency among Iraq's long-suppressed Shia majority, as well as Iraq's desire to replace Iran as the dominant Persian Gulf state. Although Iraq hoped to take advantage of Iran's revolutionary chaos and attacked without formal warning, it made only limited progress into Iran and was quickly repelled; Iran regained virtually all lost territory by June 1982.'

For the next six years, Iran was on the offensive. The war ended with neither side having made any territorial gains, and both economies in a bad state (https://en.wikipedia.org/wiki/Iran–Iraq_War (accessed 24th March 2016)).

[97] Khorramshahr had a population of about 220,000 at the outbreak of the war, with a largely wealthy, upper class population living in exclusive neighbourhoods. On 22nd September 1980 Iraq launched air strikes. Eight days of fierce fighting followed involving tanks and artillery. By 30th September the city was surrounded, and tens of thousands of Iranians were reportedly executed. The city was eventually taken on 10th November. Khorramshahr had been almost totally destroyed by Saddam Ḥussein's forces. The city became known by the Iranians as 'Khuninshahr', meaning 'City of Blood' in Farsi, because of the carnage during the war. It was eventually recaptured in April 1982.

[98] The invasion of Kuwait in August 1990 was a major conflict between Iraq and the Emirate of Kuwait, resulting in the seven-month-long Iraqi occupation of Kuwait, and direct military intervention by US-led forces in the Gulf War. The Kuwaiti military was easily defeated by the 88,000-strong Iraqi army, and the conflict was all over in three days.

[99] There is considerable variance in issues of child custody in Islam, but in more conservative Islamic states like Kuwait women have less parental rights. The chapter on Child Custody in Islamic Jurisprudence states, 'There are many reasons as to why Islam has held the father to be the legal guardian of the children — the most critical of which is remarrying. In most cases, after couples divorce they remarry. The chances of a man remarrying with children are much better than a woman with children' (http://www.al-islam.org/a-new-perspective-women-islam-fatma-saleh-moustafa-al-qazwini/chapter-5-child-custody (accessed 24th March 2016)).

[100] 'Nikāh al-mutʿah (Arabic: literally "temporary marriage"), is a type of marriage permitted in Twelver Shia Islam, where the duration of the marriage and the dowry must be specified and agreed upon in advance. It is a private contract made in a verbal or written format. A declaration of the intent to marry and an acceptance of the terms are required.' This temporary marriage is not accepted in Sunni Islam. Sunni scholars argue that it was forbidden by the Prophet Mohammed.

(https://en.wikipedia.org/wiki/Nikah_mut%E2%80%98ah.(accessed 24th March 2016))

[101] 'Under Iran's interpretation of Islamic Sharia law, in force since its 1979 revolution, adultery is punished by the stoning of convicted adulterers. Women are buried up to their shoulders, but men only up to their waists. They are spared if they manage to free themselves before dying' (http://www.telegraph.co.uk/news/worldnews/middleeast/iran/10089270/Iran-amends-law-on-stoning-for-adultery.html (accessed March 24th 2016)). However, in order to restore family honour, the spouse and/or family may carry out their own sentence before any official trial takes place.

[102] Also known as rials, and worth around £300 at the time.

[103] British judges often have little understanding of foreign cultural norms, and some seem to assume that everything should be done 'the British way'. Surely, when people's lives are at stake, a judge should seek clarification or corroboration from an expert witness before dismissing an argument as fabrication?

[104] At the very least, any rational person has to question two things about this 'dawn raid'. Firstly, why is it necessary to strip people of all dignity by refusing to let them get dressed and pack essential items? And secondly, why is it necessary to have eight uniformed officers arrest one woman who has never committed a crime? You would think she was an armed robber!

[105] For more information about mistreatment of detainees with medical conditions, go to http://www.medicaljustice.org.uk (accessed 24th March 2016). Medical Justice is an excellent small charity working exclusively with immigration detainees. It arranges for independent volunteer doctors to visit 1,000 detainees a year. The doctors document detainees' scars of torture and challenge medical mistreatment, including lack of medication and access to hospital. They challenge the Home Office to secure lasting change, and where that fails, may litigate. They also provide lawyers with evidence of systemic healthcare failures.

[106] One wonders what would have happened if Mary had been held for longer in detention. Would she have lost her eye, or worse? Every year there are avoidable deaths in immigration detention. Unlike the criminal justice system, where sentences have time limits, immigration

detention has no time limit. Whereas most European countries have now moved to a time limit and have reduced the number of immigration detainees, the UK stubbornly refuses to do either. If you want to know more or get involved in lobbying for change, look up Detention Action: http://detentionaction.org.uk (accessed 24th March 2016).

[107] Section 95 support is shared accommodation and £36.95 per week in cash.

[108] See footnote 49.

[109] City of Sanctuary is a national charity with many local member groups committed to welcome and integration for those seeking sanctuary in the UK (http://cityofsanctuary.org (accessed 24th March 2016)).

[110] Many judges have little understanding of what constitutes a genuine Christian faith. Whereas they may accept the expert witness of a medical professional, they often ignore the testimony of a minister of religion. Recently a convert was asked to name the 12 disciples. If that is the test of a whether or not someone is a Christian, then 95 per cent of churchgoers in the UK would fail it!

[111] This is a typical reaction as the reporting date (often monthly or six-monthly) approaches. Some asylum seekers are so afraid of attending the reporting centre that they don't sleep for days in advance. Often new clients at Boaz are not reporting when they come to us, and it takes a lot of TLC and patient persuasion before they are ready to do so.

[112] Key to the work of the Boaz Trust are the caseworkers or support workers. Like Bénédicte Bosman before her, Katie Lifford is the immediate point of contact with the female clients, and should take credit for much of the improvement in client well-being.

[113] See footnote 22.

Sheikh's story

I was born in Lahore, in Pakistan, in 1953. I have four brothers and one sister. My parents were Ahmadis,[114] like most of my relatives. To put this into context, 1953 was the same year that there were a series of violent riots against the Ahmadiyya Movement, mainly in the city of Lahore as well as the rest of Punjab, which were eventually quelled by the Pakistan Army. The demonstrations began in February, soon escalating into citywide incidents, including looting, arson and the murder of somewhere between 200 and 2,000 Ahmadis, while thousands more were left displaced. Unable to contain the increasingly widespread civil disorder, Governor-General Ghulam Muhammad handed over the administration of the city to the army under Lieutenant General Azam Khan, imposing martial law on 6th March.

My father had a good job as a labour officer in the Pakistan Mint, printing money. His hobby was electrical engineering, and he did a City and Guilds course on the radio. They did everything via radio at that time. I used to learn from him how to repair radios. Back then they had tubes – they were transistor radios. Then came TV, and I learned about that too. After I left school I went to college to do a diploma in Electrical Engineering.

When I was a child in school many people tried to discredit us. They said that Ahmadis were bad people. They really hated us. In Pakistan, Ahmadis are a real minority, but it's difficult to say how many Ahmadis there are, because everyone is afraid and wants to be safe, so some people don't declare it. But *we* wanted to be straightforward. We didn't want to lie and deny it. We couldn't hide it, because we had a mosque, and the congregation would go there to pray five times a day.

My father had a lot of health problems, and he died when I was 16 years old. My older brother had also done a diploma in electrical engineering. He was already working, but he didn't have a good job, so I also had to get a job to help support my family. I was working in my electronic workshop business when all the trouble started for me in my country.

During the Bhutto Government the mullahs started to demand restrictions. The 1974 anti-Ahmadiyya riots were the single largest killing and looting of Ahmadi Muslims in Pakistan's history. The Islamist parties and some mainstream parties sided together to persecute Ahmadis. They wanted to make our law stricter, and make Ahmadis kafir[115] by changing the law in the Assembly. There were 73 sects of Islam (included Ahmadis) in Pakistan, but Sunni, Shia and all the others came together against us. They stuck together in the Assembly; the Bhutto government supported them, and the law[116] was passed. I was about 21 at the time.

When I went to the mosque after that, people would throw stones. The real believers didn't stop going. Many times they attacked us. People got shot because they were considered *kafir*. One time when I was at the repair shop, many people came, and they took all the electrical appliances and tools. They took everything – didn't even leave a penny. I was there. I saw it all. I didn't want to run away, but God blessed me, and I escaped. After that I joined a big spare parts business until I could open another shop.

Even when you applied for a passport or an ID card, you were asked if you were Ahmadi, and if you said yes, they wrote it in your ID card and you had to sign it. They didn't do that for any other sect – just Ahmadis.

I got married to Iffat in 1975, and we had three sons and one daughter.

In 1977 General Zia-ul-Haq[117] came to power. He dissolved Bhutto's Assembly and declared martial law. He was very much against us and with the mullahs. Between 1980 and 1986, several new sections[118] were added to the constitution by the military government. One time, in 1991 my older son, Kaleem Waseem, who was in the ninth class at school, was kidnapped when he was going to school. Somebody came to our home and told us what had happened. He had seen a man kidnap my son on the path to the cemetery, and he got three other men to help him. They caught the man, and my son was safe. The man who did it was a member of the 'seven star' group.

A policeman that I knew came, and we went to the police station where I made an FIR, a First Investigation Report. There was a lot of pressure not to do anything. I had a relative who was the superintendent of police, but he wasn't Ahmadi. I went to see him to tell him about the problem, and he advised me not to stay in that place but to move away because that group was very bad. So we moved from Shahdara to live in Ghulshan-e-Ravi in Lahore, about ten miles away. My two sons and my daughter moved school too, because of the other pupils.

We didn't move the shop because we had spent a lot of money on it, but after that my business went downhill. I suffered a lot of trouble for about two or three years. There were a lot of threats. They said they were going to kill me, and they kept telling me to leave the shop. I was scared: something could have happened at any time. But I still kept working over there.

Then one day, on 2nd August 2003, five people came to the shop and looted it. At that time I was selling mobile phones. They took everything, even the petty cash, at gunpoint. Then 15 days later they came again. I don't know if it was the same people. Fortunately I was not there. They tried to grab my older son, Kaleem Waseem, who was outside of the shop, but he ran away. They fired at him, and the bullet grazed the back of his leg, splitting his pants and giving him a minor injury. My youngest son, Sheikh Farrukh Waseem, was inside the shop and he shut the door on them to stop them getting in. However, they fired directly at my son. The glass on the shop door was broken and one bullet was embedded in the heel of his shoe. After that he ran away. They were sitting in a three-wheel car (we call it a rickshaw in Pakistan) and shooting at him. They kept shooting, and although there were more than 100 people around at the time, no one came to help him.

After a while they stopped shooting because there was a problem with the gun, and he got away. Fortunately God helped us.

At that time I was the finance secretary of the Tajaran committee of businessmen: they called the police and pressurised them, asking, 'Why did that situation happen?' They ordered the police to make an FIR. They made an FIR but nothing happened about it.

After that we hired a security guard for the shop. When he was there, we were safe. However, the calls kept coming. The police kept telling us there was just one solution: 'Leave your religion.' My son Kaleem Waseem was taken again. This time it was the police that did it. I went and made a complaint, but they said they couldn't do anything. I had to pay to get him released.

After that we got threatening calls every week. They kept telling me to leave the country or they would kill me. Once someone on a motorcycle tried to stop my car, but I got away. Then the calls were coming every day. That was when I decided to leave the country.

In 2005 I applied for a visa, but at first I was unsuccessful. I was refused several times. Then I applied for a medical visa, because I was blind in one eye and wanted to get it repaired. I couldn't see a doctor in Pakistan because of what had happened. I didn't want to leave my children or wife at home while I was in hospital. This time the application was successful.

I could only get a visa for myself – I was lucky to get that. I couldn't bring my wife and children. I flew to Heathrow Airport and stayed with friends near the mosque in London. I didn't seek asylum – I didn't know anything about the system. I asked my friends and they said, 'If you claim asylum, they will send you back home.' Some people told me they had been waiting for four years. Some told me they had been refused. They said, 'If you claim asylum now, they will quickly send you home.' Others said, 'No, you should claim asylum.' I didn't know my rights or what the system was, and I was afraid, so I didn't claim straight away.

After I came to the UK my wife and son were attacked again in August 2005. They were coming home from the market when some of the mullahs attacked my son with a knife, but he got away. He phoned me to tell me not to come back to Pakistan because circumstances were getting worse.[119]

In the end I claimed asylum on 12th August 2005. They called me, so I went to Croydon for an interview. I was very afraid that they would send me back, and didn't know what would happen to me if they did that, but I went. I sat there all day. Three or four people told me they would catch[120] me first and put me in prison[121] in handcuffs, then decide what to do. They said that was the system.[122] The policy was very strict at that time.

At about eight or nine o'clock in the evening I was taken to a hotel in London. I stayed there about 10 to 15 days. Then they called me again. They came and caught all the people except me and two others. They put me in a car with two other asylum seekers, who were brother and sister, and took us to Liverpool.

Unfortunately one guy advised me, 'This solicitor is good. Join this solicitor.'[123]

135

When I joined this solicitor, he said, 'You are Ahmadi? You don't have any problem over there in Pakistan! Why are you claiming asylum? You can go home!'[124]

Before my Home Office interview in Liverpool I called my solicitor and told him that I had the FIR, and asked him to help me with the translation. He said he couldn't do that, so I asked him where I should go for help. He told me to go to Refugee Action in Liverpool. I went there immediately because I only had one week before the hearing. The lady from Refugee Action told me to go back to the solicitor: she said it was his job to do that.[125] She asked me for my solicitor's number, and she called him. The lady talked to my solicitor, but I don't know what the conversation between them was. However, my feeling was that the Refugee Action lady was becoming too upset, and she gave the phone back to me. The solicitor told me, 'Leave this place quickly. They are Home Office's people.' He told me to call him when I left Refugee Action. When I called him, he told me not to go there again. He said they weren't good people, and if I had anything to do with them, my case would be finished.[126]

Because time was very short before my first interview,[127] I decided to do the translation myself in my own handwriting with the help of a friend, because my English is very poor. My language is Urdu. So I did it and took it to the Home Office, but they refused my case.[128] After that my solicitor made an appeal. Just before my hearing, he called me and said that my legal aid had been stopped. The Home Office had refused it because my case was not 50 per cent.[129] He offered to take my case to appeal for £1,200.

I chose another solicitor who was in London. He called me to say that my legal aid had been allowed.[130] I went to court for the hearing, and he wasn't there, so I rang him. I said, 'I am in court now. What are you doing?'

He said, 'Do you want me as your solicitor or the other one?'

I said, 'I want you, because of the legal aid.' He faxed the court to say he would represent me, and they fixed a date for the hearing about a month later. At the hearing I was refused again. They said that I was not an exceptional Ahmadi.[131] I wasn't a public preacher.

My Ahmadi head office got all the information about me from Pakistan, about where I had lived and what I had done, and verified that my conduct and contact with the community was good. They also verified that I used to take part in its activities, and also that I was good at fulfilling the responsibilities assigned to me and served as a voluntary preacher in Pakistan. They wrote a letter four different times with everything in. I sent it to the Home Office but that was refused too.

My solicitor told me that he had sent my appeal to a barrister. After about ten days I got a letter from the Home Office to say that time was running out, and they would stop my support because they had not received my appeal. I called my solicitor to ask him what was happening. He told me that he had been waiting to hear from the barrister, and that was why he had not put in the appeal. I told him about the Home Office letter, and he said that they could not appeal because there was no error in law in the decision.

I went to London to see my community. They told me to leave that solicitor quickly and find another one. I was due to go to the reporting centre the next day, so I found a solicitor. He told me to get my file from the other solicitor and bring it as soon as possible, and he would make the appeal. He wrote to the Home Office, saying that he was representing me, with a letter from my doctor that said I needed 15 days bed rest, along with information about my appeal.

I got the bus back home to Liverpool that night at about midnight. At nine the next morning someone knocked on my door. I opened it, and there were four people there. They said, 'Come with us.' I asked them why, and they said the Home Office were detaining me. I told them I had faxed an appeal, but they said, 'You must come. You can get the papers when you are in custody.'

I was in Home Office custody for three days in Liverpool; then on 23rd November they sent me to a removal centre near Oxford.[132] They said they were sending me home, and showed me the ticket. It was for a flight on 28th November. On that day they took me to Heathrow Airport, gave me my passport and told me to sit in the big room and wait. My solicitor was trying to get it stopped. The Ahmadi community had hired him to help me, as we couldn't get legal aid.

The flight leaving at four o'clock was stopped, but my flight was at 11 o'clock. My solicitor said it was a very critical position. Maybe they would send me back home, but he was trying. The appeal was refused again in the emergency court.

I don't know what happened, but God blessed me. At 11 o'clock the flight came, and slowly people got on until everyone was gone. I was the only one left. They did not put me on the plane. I was taken back to detention in Campsfield. My solicitor took my case to the high court and was successful in getting permission for me to stay here.[133] The judge said there were three or four errors of law.

But they did not release me. I was in detention for 45 days. It was a very difficult time. They finally released me. I came back, sleepless, to Liverpool, and got my support again.[134] Just before we went to court again, my solicitor rang to say that the company was splitting and he was setting up his own business. He wanted to know if I wanted to stay with the old company or go with him. I preferred to stay with him, because I knew him. My community paid him £1,800. I wanted to be clear that he would deal with me completely. He said, 'Why not? I've got the money.' I was with him for six months. After that he wrote a letter asking for more money. I said, 'My community gave you £1,800. Why do you want more money?' He said he would not fight my case without more money. I asked what he had done with the £1,800, and he said his previous company had not given it to him.

I went to the Citizens Advice Bureau (CAB) and explained my difficult position. They began to investigate. They wrote letter after letter to the solicitors. After they finished the investigation they said, 'This guy is bluffing. He's not a good man.' The CAB made a two-page complaint on 15th December 2006 and asked me to sign it; however, I was afraid that both solicitors would make a problem for me, so I withdrew. I didn't want to complain, because I just wanted to fight my case. That was my focus. During the investigation the solicitor from the original firm got very angry when the CAB phoned them, but later they contacted me and offered to take my case bona fide. The lawyer, Mr I,[135] took me into his confidence, so I believed him and agreed.

A few weeks later he phoned me and raised the issue of the Urdu FIRs and the translation of other documents which were not submitted before, but then he asked for money for the translation of the FIR, so it wasn't free! They wanted £350. I borrowed money from here and there until I had enough to give him to proceed with the court hearing in London. After the court hearing they sent my case to the small court for rehearing at Manchester.[136] Then Mr I asked me for another £700, so I made arrangements as before. I went to court. There were two judges there. They said, 'In your FIR there is nothing about your attack. There is no mention of your incident.' I didn't know what had happened. The court showed me my handwritten translation of the document which made it look like I had invented the attack. With all the doubt about the documents, I was refused again.

So I was in a very difficult situation again. With the help of my community I got another new solicitor in London, and put in a fresh claim. After five or six months I went to sign at Dallas Court,[137] and they caught me again without any intimation. They sent me to Manchester Airport[138] for three days, then seven days near London. After seven days my solicitor did something, and I was released again. He put in a judicial review.

After that, on 4th June 2008, my judicial review was refused with these comments: 'Permission is hereby refused. Further or renewed applications should not be a bar to removal'. On 9th July the Home Office raided my home with more than ten officials for my removal; however, I was not at home on the day and escaped.

At the same time, my wife was in a difficult position in Pakistan, so she came here too on a visitor's visa. I went to the Manchester Immigration Aid Unit to see if they could put our cases together. They told me to go to the Home Office and tell them that my wife had come, and that she would be living with me because we were putting our cases together. They said, 'No, you can't do that. You must make a new claim for asylum.' I told them that my solicitor had advised me to ask that, but they said, 'No, you are wrong.' So Iffat put in a separate claim, and they refused that too. The Immigration Advisory Service took Iffat's case, but a few weeks later they said they couldn't because of the 50 per cent rule.[139]

I went to court thinking that no one wanted to help us, so I would do the case myself. My English was a little better than previously, so I studied what happened in my case. When I checked my FIRs I found that three lines about the attack were not mentioned in the solicitor's translation.[140] They had been cut out of the English. There was no name of the translator on the document either. There were many, many mistakes. But the case was still refused.

On 16th August 2010 we were told to leave our home in Eccles. Our support was stopped. Sometimes we stayed in friends' homes from our community. Some nights we stayed outside. Our situation was very serious. I asked many people what to do. Then someone said, 'Go to the Red Cross. Maybe they can help you.' I went over to the head office in Old Trafford. One guy said to go with him. He wrote my name and told me to go on Thursday to a church[141] over there. On that day I went there with my wife, and Nigel[142] interviewed me. He said, 'We don't have anywhere at the moment for you, but in the meantime you can stay over at a hotel.'[143] We had been homeless for about 14 days in all.

We stayed in the hotel for maybe 15 days.[144] Then the lady from the Boaz Trust[145] came over in her car and brought us to a house in Moston.[146] We were there about three months. During that time Ian[147] helped to arrange some interviews, and Boaz found us a solicitor, Matthieu Culverhouse from Irwin Mitchell, to take Salford Council to court.[148] The court ordered them to give us a proper home, but Salford Council took us to a place that had just one room, a kitchen and a bathroom, and told us to live there. I told them I could not live there because of my asthma. It was a very congested place, and there was no washing machine. My wife was not well, so it was not good for us. They said we could take it or leave it: they would give us nothing else. I called our solicitor, and he told us not to take it. He told them they had to give us a more suitable property.

Then they showed us a place in a basement, but how could my wife go there with all the stairs? Again, they told us we had to take it or they would finish with us. I said, 'Do you want to kill us?'

My solicitor was a very good man and told us to wait. In the end they gave us something in Longsight. It had three rooms on the ground floor, and they agreed to put in a washing machine too. We were very happy to have a home.

We were in such a bad situation, with no money, nothing. How can you live like that in another country? The Boaz Trust helped us. Nigel brought us to Liverpool, to a hospital to assess us for disability. The weather was very bad: there was snow everywhere. It took four or five hours. The staff at Boaz are very good; they helped us all the time. They came quickly every time we called. They took us from place to place in the car many times, sometimes far away.

When Raj[149] came, he took my case and studied it. When he checked my file, he was very surprised. He said, 'Why did they do that?' He put everything together in a fresh claim. It was refused, and refused again. Then he said, 'We are not going to appeal this time. You should tell your own story yourself.'

I said, 'OK.' I wrote everything down myself, and he said it was good. It was a new document. He didn't use my previous FIRs because they had been refused many times. It included all my activities since coming to the UK, all my links, what I preached, my social work, everything. He put it together as a completely new claim and sent it off. He is a very intelligent man, a good man.

I got my positive decision on 27th February 2012. My wife was still refused, so Raj made a fresh claim for her. He contacted the Home Office many times, but got no answer. So he wrote to say they should give her support while they were thinking about her status.[150] I went to Refugee Action to ask them to help with this. They filled in the forms and sent them to the Home Office. The Home Office agreed, but said that Iffat could not live with me. Someone called to say that they were coming the next day to take her to live in Liverpool! I told him, 'This is not human rights! She is my wife!'

'Oh,' he said, 'I didn't know you were living together with your wife! I will let you know what I will do.' After a few days he came back and said they had given her a place in Radcliffe – but I was still living in the Social Services accommodation in Salford!

Later on they sent us a letter to say that they were stopping my wife's support. They said it was because she was not living in her accommodation, that she was living in her husband's house. I told them that she stayed overnight sometimes because it was near her doctor, and because she had lots of medical appointments nearby.

I went to Refugee Action to tell them that they had refused her support. I showed them my calendar. I had written on it all her appointments. The Home Office had said that she was not at home ten times: I had proof of those days on my calendar, and had written everything down.

Refugee Action arranged for a hearing in London. It was by video link to Manchester. The judge said, 'You have a sister living in Pakistan. You can ask *her* to support your wife.' Soon after, my wife got a refusal decision from the court. It said my wife's sister's husband was doing well in business and we should contact her, and she would give us support – but seven days later a letter came from the Home Office to say that the support was being continued!

Fifteen days after that they gave us status! Everything happened very quickly. The main thing is status. Everything is alright now.

I have no words to describe the asylum system, because English is not my own language. There are many things that I could say. They are dodgy people. The asylum system is not good. This is a very, very bad situation for asylum seekers. Many who are refused are honest people. The Home Office makes many mistakes and wrong statements, which I have already experienced. They don't want to give people asylum: they say they are not real asylum seekers. The Home Office has done all the same things against me which we faced in our country. Firstly they try to prove that the asylum seeker is a liar and not credible. Then they start to take away his respect, to make him humiliated and pitiable. This method allows the Home Office to crush and destroy his right to life and to deport him.

The systems in the UK are very good. They are all very good, but this asylum system… In my community there was one 70-year-old who was deaf and had no relatives in Pakistan – but they sent him back forcibly with two officials to his country and handed him over to the police station. I tried to help him, and Raj[151] did too, but after two years here they sent him back.

In my opinion the asylum system here is not right. One time I wrote to my MP in Walkden. He told me he would look at all my papers. He told me to bring everything, and I brought all the letters. He wrote to the Home Office, but they refused again. The Home Office wrote in the letter to him that I was an absconder,[152] but I had always sent a fax to the reporting centre if I was unable to come. My solicitor had written a letter to prove that. The MP wrote again, but still they refused. They even refuse when MPs write.

My middle son, Sheikh Farrukh Waseem, was brought here on 10th May 2013 by an agent, and claimed asylum. However, the Home Office put him in jail and made an innocent person into a criminal for nothing. He claimed asylum at Heathrow Airport because he was in real danger in his country and had to run away. After more than two months, they have also refused him.

A few weeks ago the solicitor from the Immigration Aid Unit said she had received a letter from our community. They had confirmed all the things which my son had claimed in his Home Office interview. And she said his case is very good, so we should write to the Home Office to withdraw their refusal, because all the verification of the attacks over there show that he is genuine. On 28th June 2010, 90 people were killed in Pakistan in a three-hour attack on the mosque, and he was there. The Home Office even accept that the FIR is genuine and original.[153] The case is going to court in April.

My other two sons are in Canada. They are both married. Only my daughter is still in Pakistan. She is bound to her husband. They have fears, but he does not want to come here because they saw what happened with our asylum case.

That was a quick summary of my story.

On 16th August 2014 I started my business here. It is going well. I sell electrical goods, kitchen appliances, microwaves, hoovers, blenders, fan heaters, many things. I do business online as well as in the shop.

First of all, I believe in God. I am happy now, because my life is going better. My health is very good now. Back then I didn't even have glasses. It was difficult to find anything. Everything is OK now. I think the Boaz Trust is doing very well, and should continue. No one wants to help asylum seekers. The Boaz organisation is very honest and proud to assist the oppressed victims. I pray for Boaz that God would strengthen and develop them more. Amen!

The duty of a solicitor

After reading Sheikh's story, you may be questioning the integrity and motives of immigration solicitors. Although there are some excellent solicitors mentioned in the seven stories, most of those mentioned do *not* cover themselves in glory, and some bring shame upon the profession. However, it's important to remember that all seven of these asylum seekers were *refused* asylum, so it may well be that those whose claims were *successful* may have been accepted because *their* solicitor did a far better job. In the UK asylum system, the role of the solicitor is absolutely crucial. In fact, for some asylum seekers it may be the difference between life and death.

In the UK we have an *adversarial* system, where clients have to prove their eligibility for refugee status, and the Home Office solicitor tries to pick holes in their arguments, much as happens in the Criminal Justice System. In Sweden, where a much larger percentage of asylum seekers are granted status, they have an *inquisitorial* system, which is, as Wikipedia explains, 'a legal system where the court or a part of the court is actively involved in investigating the facts of the case'.[154] That automatically gives the client the opportunity to tell their story, much as they are doing in this book – something that rarely, if ever, occurs in the UK system.

So, in an adversarial system, the solicitor is almost as important as the client to a case. The 'Solicitors' Regulation Authority Handbook'[155] sets out these expected outcomes on its 'Code of Conduct' page:

Outcomes – You must achieve these outcomes:

1. you treat your clients fairly;

2. you provide services to your clients in a manner which protects their interests in their matter, subject to the proper administration of justice;

3. when deciding whether to act, or terminate your instructions, you comply with the law and the Code;

4. you have the resources, skills and procedures to carry out your clients' instructions;

5. the service you provide to clients is competent, delivered in a timely manner and takes account of your clients' needs and circumstances;

6. you only enter into fee agreements with your clients that are legal, and which you consider are suitable for the client's needs and take account of the client's best interests;

7. you inform clients whether and how the services you provide are regulated and how this affects the protections available to the client;

8. clients have the benefit of your compulsory professional indemnity insurance and you do not exclude or attempt to exclude liability below the minimum level of cover required by the SRA Indemnity Insurance Rules;

9. clients are informed in writing at the outset of their matter of their right to complain and how complaints can be made;

10. clients are informed in writing, both at the time of engagement and at the conclusion of your complaints procedure, of their right to complain to the Legal Ombudsman, the time frame for doing so and full details of how to contact the Legal Ombudsman;

11. clients' complaints are dealt with promptly, fairly, openly and effectively;

12. clients are in a position to make informed decisions about the services they need, how their matter will be handled and the options available to them;

13. clients receive the best possible information, both at the time of engagement and when appropriate as their matter progresses, about the likely overall cost of their matter;

14. clients are informed of their right to challenge or complain about your bill and the circumstances in

which they may be liable to pay interest on an unpaid bill;

15. you properly account to clients for any financial benefit you receive as a result of your instructions;

16. you inform current clients if you discover any act or omission which could give rise to a claim by them against you.

It seems from Sheikh's account that many of these outcomes were breached by his legal representatives.

---

[114] 'The Ahmadiyya Muslim Community … is an Islamic religious movement founded in Punjab, British India near the end of the 19th century. It originated with the life and teachings of Mirza Ghulam Ahmad (1835–1908), who claimed to have appeared in fulfilment of the prophecies concerning the world's reformer during the end times, who was to bring about, by peaceful means, the final triumph of Islam … The adherents of the Ahmadiyya movement are referred to as Ahmadi Muslims or simply Ahmadis … The Ahmadis were among the earliest Muslim communities to arrive in Britain … Currently, the community is led by its Caliph, Mirza Masroor Ahmad, and is estimated to number between 10 and 20 million worldwide.

'The population is almost entirely contained in the single, highly organized and united movement. However, in the early history of the community, a number of Ahmadis broke away over the nature of Ahmad's prophethood and succession and formed the Lahore Ahmadiyya Movement which today represents a small fraction of all Ahmadis … Many orthodox Muslims consider the Ahmadiyya either kafirs or heretics.' (https://en.wikipedia.org/wiki/Ahmadiyya (accessed 24th March 2016)). More details can be found on the Ahmadiyya website, www.loveforallhatredfornone.org (accessed 24th March 2016).
[115] *Kafir* means non-Muslim.

[116] In 1974 anti-Ahmadiyya riots led to the Second Amendment to the Constitution of Pakistan. Islamist parties forced the Government of Pakistan under Zulfiqar Ali Bhutto to pass a new law that declared members of Ahmadiyya Muslim Community as kafirs or non-Muslims.

[117] Muhammad Zia-ul-Haq (1924–1988) was a Pakistani general who deposed Bhutto in 1977 in a military coup. He declared martial law, and in 1978 assumed the presidency, having Bhutto controversially executed in 1979.

[118] In 1984 Zia-ul-Haq was responsible for another anti-Ahmadiyya amendment which restricted the freedom of religion for Ahmadis. According to this law, any Ahmadi who calls himself Muslim or 'poses as a Muslim' is liable to three years in prison.

[119] According to The Persecution.org (a website which reports on the religious persecution of the Ahmadiyya muslim community), a large contingent of police, led by the deputy superintendent, raided two Ahmadiyya printing presses (Ziaul Islam Press and Nusrat Art Press) and the offices of Ahmadiyya Community daily paper *Al-Fazl* in Rabwah on 5th August 2005. They searched the three places and seized printed and unprinted material. They arrested the keeper of the Ziaul Islam Press, Sultan Ahmad Dogar, and sealed the three buildings. (http://www.thepersecution.org/nr/2005/august.html (accessed 24th March 2016))

[120] 'Catch' is the word most commonly used by asylum seekers instead of 'detain'. Like criminals or rabbits, asylum seekers are 'caught'.

[121] IRC or Immigration Removal Centre: no different in essence from a prison, except that most of those held have committed no crime and not had a trial before being sent there.

[122] Under the Detained Fast Track or 'DFT' system, people arriving in the UK were detained as soon as they claimed asylum. Their entire asylum claim was processed while they were locked in a high-security immigration detention centre. The process was designed for asylum claims considered to be suitable for a quick decision. However, often very little was known about the person's situation. People from countries like Jamaica, Nigeria and Pakistan were often detained on the assumption that hardly anyone from there could be a genuine asylum seeker.

In June 2015, the high court ruled that it was wrong to detain asylum seekers and accelerate their appeals. Senior judges said the DFT system did not take into account the complexity of claims, and Lord Dyson, the Master of the Rolls, said truncating the time available for appeals was 'systemically unfair'. Permission for the Home Office to appeal was denied, and DFT was suspended, although it may well be reintroduced in a different form at some stage. A detailed report of the high court's findings can be found at http://www.bbc.co.uk/news/uk-33704163 (accessed 29th March 2016).

[123] The firm, which shall remain nameless for legal reasons, was based in south-west London.

[124] Unfortunately a small minority of solicitors and interpreters are not impartial, especially when the case centres on a religion that they consider false or even blasphemous. There is a great temptation to not represent their client well or even do something to ensure their case fails.

[125] I am reliably informed that there is money in the legal aid budget for translations of important documents. At the very least the solicitor should have been able to find a translator and tell Sheikh where to take the FIR, even if he did not do that himself.

[126] If this was indeed what the solicitor told Sheikh, it was not only extremely unprofessional, but untrue. Refugee Action is a highly respected NGO that has been working on behalf of asylum seekers and refugees for many years. Far from being an agent of the government, Refugee Action is often critical of Home Office policy, and regularly lobbies for change in the asylum system (http://www.refugee-action.org.uk (accessed 24th March 2016).

[127] This was the 'Initial' or 'Substantive' Interview, and very important. As the main interview, it provides the basis of the asylum claim, and what happens there affects any subsequent appeals and submissions.

[128] Once an item has been considered and rejected, it is very difficult to get it reconsidered unless there is an error in law. If the solicitor had had the FIR correctly translated at the beginning, perhaps Sheikh would have been granted leave to remain much quicker.

[129] Applicants are only entitled to legal aid to fund representation at appeal if it is judged that their case has a 50 per cent or more chance of success. The legal advisor has to decide whether the case meets the merits test or not. Research suggests that cases may be abandoned

because advisors don't apply to the LSC for funding or funding is refused. Previous anecdotal evidence suggested cases may also be dropped based on, for example, who the adjudicator is (some adjudicators were apparently thought to be more likely to allow appeals than others). Clients who have been dropped by their advisor at the appeal stage are unlikely to be able to find another advisor to take on their case, and indeed may not be able to find someone else within the time limits.

'Legal Services Consumer Panel report', 15th October 2012, p17. (http://www.legalservicesconsumerpanel.org.uk/ourwork/vulnerablec onsumers/2012%2010%2010%20Immigration%20desk%20research%20 and%20scoping%20final.pdf (accessed 24th March 2016))

[130] This begs the question, 'If *this* solicitor was able to get legal aid, why wasn't the previous one?' And there is perhaps a supplementary question: 'Did the original solicitor inform Sheikh that there was no legal aid *as soon as* he knew that, or did he, perhaps with a nice payout in mind, wait until the appeal was imminent?'

[131] It is common for the Home Office to refuse a case on the grounds that the asylum seeker is not sufficiently 'high profile' to warrant persecution. For example, a member of a national committee may be considered a target, but not a regional activist. This demonstrates how out of touch they are with the reality of life in many countries, where merely being associated with a particular opinion or person may be extremely dangerous.

[132] Campsfield House used to be a youth detention centre, but it reopened as an Immigration Detention Centre in November 1993. It now has around 215 bed spaces for men only. Campsfield is run by the American company GEO who are responsible for immigration detention centres in the US, Australia and South Africa.

[133] This was not a positive decision on his asylum claim, merely temporary leave to remain while the case was considered.

[134] At that time asylum support rates were set at 70 per cent of Income Support. Singles aged 18-24 received £32.80 a week, and over 25s received £41.41. The tie to income support was subsequently removed, and in October 2009 the higher rate for over 25s was abolished. In 2016 the rate for all singles is £36.95, equivalent to 64 per cent of income support.

[135] This whole saga paints these legal firms in a very bad light. However, since much of the evidence of wrongdoing and unprofessional conduct rests on verbal promises and statements, it would be very difficult to prove, even if Sheikh had the backing of the CAB. Clients do have a right to complain to the Legal Ombudsman (at the time it was within six months, now extended to 12), but did they tell him that? Sheikh gave me the names of the firms and the solicitors concerned, but I have been advised, for legal reasons, not to include them in the story.

[136] Manchester Immigration and Asylum Chamber in Piccadilly.

[137] Dallas Court is the Immigration Reporting Centre in Salford that serves most of Greater Manchester. It is a grey, single-storey building on an industrial estate, well away from any residential properties. Those reporting have to queue outside, whatever the weather. There is no shelter. The nearest bus route is a quarter of a mile away, and the nearest place to park is even further away.

[138] Manchester Airport has a small Holding Centre for up to 12 immigrants. They can be held there for up to five days before being transferred to an Immigration Removal Centre.

[139] See footnote 129.

[140] One can only assume that this was a deliberate omission, either by the solicitor or perhaps the translator, to ensure that the case of an Ahmadi was unsuccessful.

[141] St Bride's Church, Old Trafford. The first Destitution Project started in Mustard Tree charity in 2003, and moved to St Bride's in 2004.

[142] Nigel Biggs was the housing manager of the Boaz Trust at the time. Thursday afternoon at St Bride's was often where we met and registered those who were destitute and in need of accommodation.

[143] At the time the Red Cross had some emergency funds set aside to accommodate destitute asylum seekers for a few days in cheap hotels in Manchester.

[144] This was far longer than normal, probably because Iffat had severe mobility issues that made it dangerous to be homeless on the streets.

[145] Jo Garbutt, who was the hosting coordinator.

[146] One reason it took so long to find a room for them was Iffat's disability. Barely able to walk, she had to have a downstairs room and access to a downstairs toilet. That house in Moston was the only Boaz Trust property that could provide those facilities. Even so, it was not

ideal to put a married couple in a house for women, but it was the only option available.

[147] Ian Pollock was a volunteer at the Boaz Trust for several years and helped a number of clients to access legal help and asylum support.

[148] The Boaz Trust had written to Salford City Council, asking them to accommodate Sheikh and Iffat in Social Services accommodation, since they had a duty of care due to Iffat's severe arthritis. They refused, so Irwin Mitchell took the case to court. The judge ruled in Sheikh and Iffat's favour.

[149] Raj Brightman, the Boaz Solicitor.

[150] Asylum seekers who make a fresh asylum claim are eligible for support if the Home Office accepts that it meets the criteria for consideration.

[151] Raj Brightman, The Boaz Trust solicitor.

[152] Most asylum seekers are required to report at the nearest Reporting Centre at regular intervals. If they do not do so, or do not provide good reasons for not attending, they are considered to be absconding. Sometimes they are accused of absconding even if they have an attendance rate over 90 per cent.

[153] There is always a Catch-22 when it comes to documents, especially from countries where corruption is rampant and bribes commonplace. On the one hand the Home Office will say, 'Where are the documents that prove what you say?', but if you produce documents they often argue that they are no proof at all because false documents can be easily bought.

[154] https://en.wikipedia.org/wiki/Inquisitorial_system (accessed 24th March 2016).

[155] http://www.sra.org.uk/solicitors/handbook/code (accessed 24th March 2016).

Kundai's story

I was born in Harare, Zimbabwe, in 1976. I was born three months premature, on 6th August, and I had a cleft lip. I was kept in an incubator and fed through a tube until I was big enough to come out and have surgery to correct the problem.

There were five children in my family: two girls and three boys. My sister Antoinette was the oldest, then there were the three boys, and I was the youngest child. My dad was a contractor in a company called Sisk, building houses and roads. Before that he had worked for a very big supermarket called Rockalls. He was one of the black men who had a very good opportunity of working with the white people when the Smith[156] regime was in charge in Zimbabwe in the seventies. My mum was a businesswoman. She used to sew clothes on her machine and sell them or give them away to less privileged people working on the farms. After that she bought a coach, which operated between Harare and Mutare in the Eastern Highlands of Zimbabwe.

My mum and dad started having problems. I don't really know what happened, because I was young, but they separated when I was about seven years old. That really was a very sad time for me. I never really had time together with my dad, and even now it affects me in some way. I remember him arguing with my mum when I was about six, then he went away for a very long time. That hurt me a lot, because I used to see other kids with their dads in school on parents' day, and *my* dad wasn't there – that was so painful. One time I said to my mum, 'Where's my dad? I need to see him.' He was working away in another part of the country with Sisk. That time he did come back.

In school I was very clever. I came first in my class. It was prize-giving day at school, and parents were there. After a while I saw my dad there. He had bought me a book, *The Three Billy Goats Gruff*. That was the first book he bought me, and I kept it for years. He said, 'I love you, and I'm going to be there for you, whatever you want. I want you to remember me every time you read this book.' That was really the last time that I saw him. So I grew up with my mum, sister and brothers. My mum never remarried. In fact, they never got divorced, just separated.

I really had a happy childhood because my mum was there for me. She provided everything for us. She was a very hard-working lady, and I think that's where I got my work ethic from. I was a privileged child growing up. There wasn't a big class divide back then, but back home we had housekeepers and garden boys. I went to boarding school, and when I came home for the holidays my mum would say, 'You need to do your washing and cooking.'

I used to cry and say, 'I don't think I am your child, because we have a housekeeper to do all that! We have a garden boy, and you are asking me to go and grow my own vegetables!' But now I am very grateful for that: she gave me a very good background, and now I know I don't need to rely on anyone else – I can rely on myself.

My memories of that time are good, really. My mum used to travel a lot, and wherever she went she would bring me back a cake from the area, whether it was Botswana or another country. At the time she was buying commodities in other countries and bringing them back to sell. She would go for weeks, but I was well looked after, and we would spend the school holidays together. She did spank me once or twice, but only when I had been naughty, like the time I set fire to a big bag of cotton wool in my bedroom. I liked experimenting: I just wanted to see how it would burn!

My mum owned a supermarket as well as grinding mills: we had quite a lot of employees. Then, in 1990, my mum fell ill. I wanted to be with her, so they took me out of boarding school. Apart from my dad leaving I had never experienced any real sadness until then.

One day we went to my uncle's house in the village. We were sitting there talking, and I was asking when I was going to see my dad, and why she wouldn't let me see him, and so on. She was sitting in a folding chair, one of those camping chairs. I don't know exactly what happened, but she fell into the fire. She was burned very badly – she had over 50 per cent burns. She was in a private hospital for ages, but she never recovered, and she died. She was only 45 years old.

The memory of what happened is still with me. I came through it with the help of a friend called Audrey, but I often blamed myself. I thought maybe it was my fault that she died, that maybe I had made her angry, and then… I don't know. It happened so quickly.

After my mum died, I was looked after by my sister. She was much older than me and was already working. I was 15 and she was 31. Because she did everything for her kids, my mum had written a will, but the lawyers wanted my dad to be present because they were still married. That was the first time I had seen my dad for ages, but that never changed anything for me, because he was still my dad. When everyone was fighting and arguing over my mum's wealth, I just was so happy to see my dad, and wanted him to have a share of it. When the others were saying that he wasn't going to get any of it, I said he could have some of my share. My uncles kept saying that would have made my mum sad, because she was doing it for her kids, but I said that didn't matter. When my parents split and the house was sold, my dad didn't get anything from that, so he should have had a right to some of it. Anyway, the courts ruled that he should oversee it all, along with my sister, as he had never divorced my mum.

So I was still living a happy life, even without my mum, and began to rebuild my relationship with my dad. But I still had a lot of unanswered questions, like why he never wrote me a letter or even a postcard. It wasn't like he couldn't afford it – we were well off.

I kept going to school and then went on to college. I always wanted to do catering. My mum used to have quite a lot of friends coming round, and I grew up with a lot of white Zimbabweans too. She used to do a lot of entertaining, and was very generous. She would see a stranger sitting by the side of the road and invite them in.

We had a big house with seven bedrooms. I remember one day that my mum brought in a woman and her two kids. She was having a problem with her husband, and I remember my mum saying, 'Kundai, you need to give up your bedroom and share with me.' I cried because I had my own bedroom. She gave my bedroom to the lady and her children, and told me I could either share with her or sleep in the living room. Because of this I asked her if I really was her child: I had always wondered, because I am darker than my siblings, and was born six years after Nicholas. I thought maybe I was adopted!

My mum used to bring in homeless orphans too: I never thought something like that would happen to me one day, 25 years later. Like they say, 'What goes around, comes around.' Some of the people she used to help – refugees, really – were from countries like Malawi, Mozambique and Zambia: countries that were not good like Zimbabwe. Back then, Zimbabwe was known as the bread basket of Africa.

Then I went to college to do catering and hotel management. At home I used to cook a lot. I loved to sing and dance too, and my sister thought I would be a singer, but every weekend I would cook for people coming round, and cooking won out in the end.

Then, when I was 19, I met a guy called Packham at the college, and we started going out and dating. My mum had always said that I should keep my purity for the right man. She used to say, 'There is nothing as precious as giving your purity to your husband.' I had been brought up in the Catholic Church, but then I left to go to a Pentecostal church for a while. I believed in God, and we used to fast and pray every Monday, not just in the church but at boarding school too. We fasted so we would have a good week. We even fasted for the first ten days of every New Year. It became like a ritual really.

I had kept myself pure like my mum had said, but then I thought that Packham was the right one for me, and I fell pregnant with Lynna while I was still studying. I had won a bursary to go to one of the best catering schools in Switzerland, but I couldn't go because I was pregnant. I kept on going to college: no one knew I was pregnant, because I was hiding it. I didn't want to be expelled.

When it came to my last year we had to do practical placements in hotels. You had to choose three five-star hotels. By then people knew I was pregnant. I got offered one of the best hotels, in Victoria near the falls – one that everyone wanted. There were lots of Americans and Canadians visiting there, and going white-water rafting. If someone let it out about the pregnancy, that would have been the end of my placement, but my sister wanted me to go as far as I could. My due date was 24th July 1997, and I was due to start work on 1st August, but the baby didn't come until 8th August.

My sister Antoinette rang and told the hotel that I wasn't well. She asked if they would keep my place for a few weeks. Then I got a letter from the college asking me to come in, because they had heard that I was pregnant. He gave me a date to come in on 5th. I gave birth on the 8th and came out of hospital two days later. My sister phoned the hotel and told them I had had malaria but was better now. Then she sent me off to the hotel, and I started my placement while Antoinette looked after baby Lynna. The deputy head of my course came over to check, and thought that everyone had been lying about my pregnancy. After a few weeks Antoinette offered to keep looking after Lynna so that I could finish my education. She hadn't been able to have any children of her own, so looking after Lynna was like a blessing in disguise for her.

When I finished my course I got a job as a receptionist in a hotel. This was the start of the troubles that led to me fleeing Zimbabwe and ending up here in England. At that time I had no intention whatsoever of coming to England. If I had a choice of any country, I would have gone to Switzerland to do my Higher Diploma as a chef. That was my passion. Sometimes God has a different plan for our destiny, and we don't know it, but it's in our circumstances.

It all started when Mugabe's[157] supporters started taking farms from white people.[158] My sister was a war veteran who had fought for Zimbabwe in the eighties. She went with Sally Mugabe, who was then Robert Mugabe's wife. She was a policewoman, then joined the ministry of defence, so her livelihood came from Mugabe. I was 20 by now, and knew what was right and what I wanted. I began to get involved with ZAPU,[159] when Tekere was there, then with the MDC[160] under Tsvangirai. I didn't think it was right for the white farmers to get their farms taken off them and be chased out of Zimbabwe. Their great-grandfathers had come over here, and they knew nothing except being white Zimbabweans. Why should they suffer for things that happened 50 years ago? And why would you take a farm from someone who has all the farming knowledge and give it to someone like me who only knows how to grow enough for my family?

It began to cause problems between me and my sister, because she was well known in ZANU-PF. Even my mother had been a chairwoman in the party. I used to go to the MDC campaigns, and joined in with everybody, but I didn't know how bad things would get. One day I was coming home from work. The hotel owner had something to do with ZANU-PF, and all the other guys working on reception were ZANU-PF supporters except for me and one of the managers, who came to England before I did.

There was a campaign to get everyone to go to the Sheraton Hotel, where Mugabe was staying, for a rally in support of ZANU-PF. No one had to work on the day of the rally, but I was working. I was taking bookings, so they knew I was at work. Then an army of men came to the hotel and asked for me to come out, because I was an MDC supporter. The manager came out and told them I wasn't there, but they said they knew I was, because they had rung and I had answered the phone. She tried to hide me, but they threatened to burn down the hotel if I didn't come out. I could see that there were more than 50 customers in there, and I knew the men would do what they threatened, so I decided to go out to them. They dragged me all the way from the hotel to the Sheraton. They called me names, and at one point I was so scared that I thought they were going to rape me.

When we got there all the MDC supporters were surrounded. They told us we were going to stop what we were doing, and made us shout the ZANU-PF slogans. I didn't want to do that. They beat some people up, and tear gas was thrown too. I couldn't breathe or see anything.

They took a group of us to Harare Central Police Station. We sat on the floor. I was so scared that I wouldn't get out of there, so I rang my sister and begged her to help me. She refused to help me and told me I had to do that myself. She said she had tried to tell me that what I was doing wasn't right. I had made my own bed and now I had to lie in it. I thought she was abandoning me: I thought maybe it was because she was a ZANU-PF supporter, or maybe she was doing that to protect her family, but really I had no idea why she was acting like that.

I was there overnight with no food and no blankets. They were shouting at us and being horrible. I didn't know who to ring, but then I thought about a friend of my sister. He came over and paid a fine of 100 dollars, and they let me out. They also told me to swear that I would never again be part of MDC. I did, just so they would release me, but I never stopped.

Then I moved to a place of my own. I took Lynna, but after a while she went back to live with my sister, and I went back to work. I was being followed all the time, and there was no peace. One of the managers, Christa Kalulu, who is now a government minister in Zambia, knew what was going on. She said to me, 'Kundai, you need to go somewhere until things are alright. If you don't go, they are going to kill you. They will imprison you, or your family will suffer.'

I thought, 'What am I going to do? Where am I going to go?' Christa rang my sister, who came over. We started talking, and I asked my sister why she hadn't helped me. She said that she had known what was going on, and if she had got involved, it would have been bad for me, the family and Lynna. She was protecting me from what had happened to her years before, when she had been put in jail for a couple of years.

Christa Kalulu said she knew people in high places of authority, and could arrange everything for me to get out. She said I could go to England, because she knew some people there. I said, 'Why not South Africa until it calms down?', but she said that was too near – Mugabe had his accomplices there too. Even going to another African country wouldn't work.

She did arrange it all, and I came over to the UK on 27th August 2000. I didn't need a visa, and I didn't know how to claim asylum. She just said, 'You'll be fine when you get there. I've got people there who will help you.' When I arrived at Manchester Airport the immigration officer asked me why I was there. He was very friendly. I showed the official my passport and the letter Christa had given me, and he stamped the passport with a visa for six months. He asked me if I had anyone waiting for me, and I said yes.

At first I went to stay with someone Christa had arranged. I was there three months, and then I got in touch with my eldest cousin, Abigail, and I stayed with her. Back then most people in Zimbabwe didn't know about seeking asylum. It was only a month before my visa ran out when we started looking for solicitors. I went to a solicitor[161] in North Manchester with all my documents. Mr S took all the documents, and said he would help me with my asylum claim.

It was quiet for well over six months. I heard nothing, so I went over to see the solicitor to find out what was going on. He said the Home Office had received the documents and I would get an acknowledgement. It was a while before that letter came, and then about a year after I applied I got another letter saying that my application had been refused because I was an 'overstayer'. They were saying that I was classified as an absconder because I had not left after the six months when my visa expired, and that I would have to leave the country.

When I had my interview at Dallas Court the lawyer who came to represent me was not the same guy who was there the first time. I was asked all sorts of questions about how and why I came here, and after that I was asked to fill in a declaration form. The solicitor told me I didn't need to answer any of the questions. He said, 'You just remain quiet, and I will do the talking for you. You just sign when they ask you to.'

Looking back now I wish that I had said to the immigration officer, 'Can I read what you have written down?' because I don't know what he wrote down. I didn't have a copy. He could have written anything there.

I felt like my solicitor had let me down. I was angry. I had put in my asylum claim a month before my visa expired, and then that happened. After I got the refusal letter, Mr S told me that I should move away from my cousin's house, because the immigration officers might come and take me if I stayed there. But I didn't know where I could go.

Then I got a letter from Dallas Court to say that I had to go and sign there every week. I did that, like they said. My solicitor put in an appeal against my refusal, and I had to go to court on 21st July 2001. My solicitor said, 'Don't worry. You don't need to go. You don't need to be present. I can give them the facts.' So I didn't go, in the hope that he would represent me. Then I got a letter from the Home Office that said no one had represented me on the day. I have got a copy of the letter.

If I had gone and pleaded my case, maybe things would have been different. I don't know, but now I am seeing things in a different way. Maybe you need to go through a journey in life. It was through that journey that I came to have a really good relationship with God. I can see now that God was with me, and if I hadn't gone through that I wouldn't be appreciating what I have now. Sometimes you have to go through a journey to appreciate things in life and see the hand of God.

Some people I know were caught[162] walking down the street or were taken from their houses, but that never happened to me. I just stayed in the country. They had my passport until it expired in 2004. I eventually got it back in 2010 when I got my leave to remain.

I think there were three appeals altogether. The second one, they said I didn't have enough evidence, even though I was still participating in the MDC – I never stopped doing that. I used to go to Hulme, where they had meetings every weekend. I was also part of the Zimbabwean Association group that used to go to London for campaigns and stuff. Thomas Date was the leader. We used to meet up near One Central in Manchester every Friday to discuss things and see how we could help people, find solicitors and so on. I thought, 'Why should I stop? We still need to help people in Zimbabwe.'

I was living like a ghost. The Zimbabwean Association would give people five or ten pounds, and I was living with friends who were working. Then I met an English guy called Marvin*, who became my boyfriend.

Sometimes you do things because you just want to be safe. You just want someone to look after you, and it's so hard when you have nothing. And sometimes you can be a burden to people, no matter how much they want to help you. You feel like you are in their way; they can't have their own privacy, and you feel like you are eating all their food. Then, when you just want to sit down sometimes and think about the things that are going on in your life, they think that you are being moody. People don't really understand, and it was becoming really hard for me, until I met Marvin. I felt that I had met someone who loved me just for myself, so we moved in together. He just accepted me for who I am. I was honest with him about everything – just laid it on the table. We lived together, and he was trying to help me out. I met his family, and we were together for nearly six years. He was looking after me, giving me everything I needed.

Marvin looked online to see who could help with my case, and someone referred us to the North Manchester Law Centre in Harpurhey, where there was a drop-in. That was the nearest to us, as we were living in Whitefield. The solicitor there said that he would help. Then he told Marvin that if they knew he was keeping an illegal immigrant,[163] it would be considered a crime. He then advised us that, as I could not reapply for asylum, our best option was to get married, since we had been together for a long time. That was the only way I could stay in the

168

country. As it was, I would be classified as a common wife after being together for so long. He said he would give us a form so we could apply to get married. He said they may ask you to go and get married in your own country, and then you could get married here.[164]

But for me, for some reason, that was something I didn't believe in: marrying for convenience. I didn't want that. It wasn't right. Even though I didn't have any hope, any other way or plan B, I didn't want to do that. We started going to the Church of England, because he said, 'If you do that, it's well known and you register yourself. You go every Sunday, and that's where you can marry. The government will believe that.' So we started doing that, but there was something in me that was telling me that it wasn't right. I didn't know what it was. We got engaged, and we did love each other, but I didn't want to marry for convenience just to stay in the country.

I told Marvin that I didn't think it was right. I had been going to a church in Stockport. They kept saying that you shouldn't be with someone who wasn't of the same belief or colour. They were very restrictive, so I stopped going there, and we went to the Church of England in Crumpsall. The minister there was from South Africa. We sort of clicked because he knew what was going on in Zimbabwe.

It still didn't feel right, and I began to feel that I was with Marvin for the wrong reasons. When I told him that I didn't think it was right to get married, his whole family turned against me. They said I could make it work if I wanted. Marvin and I started having problems, arguing. His sisters were saying that I would be on my own and have nothing if I left him, and no one would help me.

I felt trapped: I was so scared. I thought he was the only one who could be there for me. Even if he was rough with me, I said to myself, 'It doesn't matter – he looks after me.' Even when he or his sisters were abusive, I had no one else, so I stayed there. He had a hold on me really. If I did anything wrong, they would say, 'We can call immigration or the police, and they will come and take you.' That frightened me. I had been going to Dallas Court, but there came a time when I stopped. I was scared, because people had been caught.

Then in September 2009 things really took a turn for the worse. Things were really bad between me and Marvin. We had a big argument, and somehow the fear was taken off me. I said, 'You know what, Marvin? I don't need you. I came into this country on my own. I know I've been with you, but I've had enough. I don't know what it is, but I'm going to find my own way out there.'

His sister Jackie said, 'You'll be back.'

I told her, 'I'm not coming back. My path and his are not going to cross ever again.' I didn't have a clue what I was going to do or where I was going to go, but I found the strength and walked out – with nothing. I left everything behind, all the clothes he had been buying for me, everything.

It was a Friday night. I walked all the way from Whitefield to Victoria Station. I didn't know who to call. My cousin didn't want to know, because she was afraid that, if Immigration came, they would think she was hiding me. I was sitting in Victoria Station with the trams going past. It looked like I was waiting for a tram, until they stopped running. I didn't know where I could sleep, so I walked up to the station office. There was a guy there; unfortunately I didn't get his name, but I still remember him. I went and sat down. He said, 'Are you ok?'

I said, 'Not really. I have just split up with my boyfriend, and I have nowhere to go.'

He invited me into his office and made me a cup of tea. He let me stay there until the morning, and then he said to me, 'You know, there is a place in Hulme that helps people in your situation. I can look it up for you and you can go there.'

I told him I didn't have any bus fare, but he gave me the money to get there.

I was the first there: it was probably only about six o'clock in the morning. It was still dark, and people were looking at me as they passed by. Then I saw other people coming: a guy from Iraq, then one from Eritrea. He told me he had been coming for a while, and there was a guy called Tony who helped people. The place was called ASHA.[165] The queue kept getting longer, until the doors opened. I filled in the registration form, then saw Tony. He told me there were a lot of Zimbabweans in the same situation as me, as well as lots of other nationalities. That was how I came to know about Boaz. Tony said there was a place called Boaz that housed destitute asylum seekers, and another place called WAST[166] for women, where you could talk. At WAST Vicki was there for me, and I could offload anything and everything. There were other women in relationships because they had no one to look after them. They hadn't got into those relationships because they wanted to, but because they would be out in the rain if they didn't.

Vicki asked me if I wanted to report any of the abuse, but I said no, I didn't want to get anyone in trouble. She said I could go to her house and stay there. I stayed overnight, but the next day she asked me if I was signing, and I said no. She told me that I couldn't stay any longer because her husband worked at Dallas Court. I thought my world was falling in again, but I wasn't going to go back to Marvin and grovel.

Jo Garbutt from Boaz came over. She said that she would have taken me, but she and her husband David were going on holiday for a week. She took me to stay with a couple in Chorlton until they got back. I stayed with Karl and Sally for two nights, and then moved over the road to their friends Steve and Margaret for a while. I was there over Christmas 2009, and they were very kind. It felt like I was part of their family. I was there for a month or two, then I went to live with David and Jo, where I stayed for about six months.

I often think back to the time when I got angry with my mum for putting an asylum seeker in my room and inviting strangers into our house. I never imagined that would one day be me, living as a stranger in someone else's house. I was now the refugee in a foreign country, being provided with food and a roof over my head without paying anything. What my mum used to do for others was now happening to me.

When I lived with David and Jo I was introduced to Boaz. I met other people living in Boaz houses, and I remember coming to the Boaz office some days and meeting people who were in the same boat as me, although we had all had different circumstances and journeys in our

172

lives. It gave me something to look forward to every week, meeting other people and making friends. I went to the sewing and craft classes. When you are waiting for your case to be dealt with, or when you have been refused, you can't work or do anything. Having Boaz gave me something to do, making my time useful. Some of the people who come to this country are really skilful people. They had jobs before, but then you can't work when you get here. You are just sitting there: you can't practise anything. You lose touch with things you used to do, and if you aren't allowed to go to college, you lose everything – so Boaz was so helpful, because you could fill your time with good things.[167]

I was also going to the foodbank on a Thursday at St Bride's church and meeting other people there who understood what I was going through. You could open up and talk to them, because they had been through the same things. It's good to know you are not on your own. Other people can understand up to a certain point, but there are some things that you can't share with them – you can only share them with people who have been through the same things.

There was an adviser at Boaz called Ian, who looked at my case. I was also going to WAST, where we had access to computers so we could help ourselves with our cases, and going to ASHA to see Tony Openshaw. People told me he was very good at his job, but I had lost hope really.

Maybe the reason that I went through all that journey was so that I would be grateful for all the things that God has done for me. I stayed in the country from 2000 until 2010, while other people were caught walking down the street, or working. Some were sent to detention. Some were sent back home. Some went to Dallas Court and never came back. Vicky used to tell us, 'Try to go with someone, in case they grab you – then they can come and tell us.' I used to think I was just lucky, but now I can see it was the hand of God that it never happened to me. There was a purpose in my life. Although I was brought up as a Christian, I didn't really have an identity in Jesus. I had been relying on myself before, and had been trying to figure out things for myself without God. That's hard. But David and Jo had introduced me to South Manchester Family Church, and I knew that it was a place where I really belonged. I felt welcomed. I felt at home. I felt that I had an extended family that I had never had before. I always say to myself, 'If I had known back then the God that I know now, maybe things would have been different.'

Before then my relationship with God had not been deep. I had been going to church and had been praying, but had never had the deep relationship with God that I had always wanted. But now I gave everything to God. When you surrender everything to Him, and let Him be in charge, and stop struggling and fighting with Him, if it's His will, He can make things right, but He needs that platform in your life.

I always wanted to go to church and do the right thing, but I'm a human being, and I fail. I was trying to find the way. Being part of the church and getting to know people gave me something to look forward to. Living with David and Jo and being part of a house group was amazing.

Even now I am someone who lives in a bubble. I don't let many people into my bubble because I am afraid that, if

I get really close to someone and I love them a lot, I will lose those people. I always ask myself why it is that all the people I love, the people who understand me and I can share with, are taken away, and I blame myself for that. Sometimes I come across as someone who is not friendly or open, but when I am with the people I have let into my bubble, I feel relaxed and able to share.

I have always had this fight in me, this strength: I wasn't just going to wait and sulk because I couldn't work, so when I was at David and Jo's I started to look around and see what options I had. I wanted to do something with my life, not just rely on other people. I didn't want to be a charity case. It was already embedded in me by my mum that you had to work hard for your living. Even if I was going to be sent back home, I wanted to go back with something that I could use for the future. I had already been out of work for eight years. My English was quite good, so I didn't need to go to college for that, but now that I knew I had a purpose in my life and I could trust in God, I knew that everything would come out right. I placed everything in His hands.

Tony Openshaw helped me put together a fresh claim for asylum; then he put in an application for me to get Section 4 housing, and that was successful. They gave me a place in a shared house in Bolton. I remember the date because it was my birthday, 5th August 2009. We were also given vouchers for the supermarket, but you could only use them for certain things like food and clothes. It gave me a different perspective on things, and made me treasure the things I have. I was able to buy enough food for the week. I was living on limited resources, but I was like a king compared to other people, and I was so grateful to the government for the accommodation and food.

I was advised to go to the Immigration Aid Unit, but they couldn't take my case because they didn't have enough government funding, but the Immigration Advisory Service in Salford agreed to take it on, as they had funding to take on some legacy cases.[168]

When I was living in Bolton I told Linda from our church about my passion for being a chef. At that time she was teaching at Bolton College, and she told me about it. I didn't think much more about it, but one day I decided to go and visit Bolton College. I explained to the receptionist that I was an asylum seeker, and that I had a passion to be a chef. The lady told me that they didn't have a programme like that for asylum seekers, but suggested that I came back on Wednesday to talk to one of the administrators. She told me that there was a fund for asylum seekers to attend college. The fund wasn't actually for what I wanted to do, but maybe they could help. When I went back on Wednesday, they asked me to bring in all my catering certificates, Home Office documents and ID. They accepted me for the course, and I studied there for a year.

The reason I say that it was all in God's plan is that I finished my course on 4th July 2010, and on July 10th my solicitor rang me. I was in Bolton train station waiting for a train to Manchester when the call came. She said, 'I've got news for you', but she didn't say 'good news', and my heart sank.

I said, 'Is it good or is it bad?'

She said, 'Are you sitting or are you standing?' I thought that meant it was bad news, but then she said, 'I just want to say "Congratulations!"' In my head I thought maybe I would get what a lot of other people were getting – two and a half years or five years leave to remain, but then she said, 'You've been given indefinite leave to remain.' I couldn't believe it. I started jumping up and down on the platform and singing praises to God.

I got straight on the phone and told Jo Garbutt (from Boaz). I was *so* happy. I couldn't believe it and even doubted it was true until I saw the papers. I picked them up on my birthday, 5th August, after the solicitor had come back from holiday. To be honest, it took me two years to properly realise that I was now free. I was always looking over my shoulder, and I was still scared to do some things in case it was against the law or I would be in trouble. I still thought that I could jeopardise my stay if I did something wrong.

As soon as I got my papers I wanted to work. I didn't want to go on benefits. I got a CV done for me, and went looking for a job. I went everywhere with my CV, after all kinds of hotel jobs, from washing dishes to cleaning toilets. I still had my asylum benefits for about a month, so that kept me going, and then I was able to get working tax credits. When I went to the Britannia Hotel, where the manager had been so good to me on my college placement, they didn't ask me to do a week's work trial, but just one day. They took me on, and my first day in permanent employment as a chef was on 24th November 2010.

It felt like everything had been planned for me by God. Everything was falling into place: finishing college, getting my papers and then getting my job. The whole process has made me realise that everything is in God's time and timing. We may want to rush things, but He has His own timing.

I still had to find somewhere to live, though, because I could only stay in my accommodation in Bolton for a month after being granted leave to remain, because someone else needed to move in. Thankfully the agency that owned the Bolton house had another property in Salford, and they said I could go there. They let me stay there for almost a month without paying; then I was able to move into a basement flat owned by a friend in Burnage. I was there for about a year. When I started at Britannia I didn't have any money, so I used to walk the whole way to work every day. I did that for about a month until my first wages came through. I didn't want to borrow money, because I needed it to save up for a proper place of my own, and I also needed it to send home for Lynna.

I worked for Britannia for just over a year. By then I was ready for a new challenge. I wanted to improve myself, and I found a job at what was then the Linen restaurant in the Manchester 235 Casino. I started there on 10th January 2012. Soon after that James Martin took it over and it became James Martin Manchester. By then I was earning £7.50 an hour, but I didn't have enough savings to bring Lynna over – I only had about £500 saved.

After my sister died back in 2009, my cousin had looked after Lynna, who was 12 years old, but things there were not good. They used to abuse her physically, and it was so painful for me because there was nothing that I could do – I was so far away. I managed to send money back for her, but if I failed to do that they would take it out on her. I was earning £242 a week at the time after tax, and my rent was

178

£300 a month, so I was able save up enough for a deposit for a bigger place to live.

The first time I applied for Lynna to come and join me here, they said that I wasn't earning enough, and also that my place wasn't big enough for two – I needed to have two bedrooms or a bedroom and a living room that could count as a bedroom. They said that I needed to be earning over £18,000 a year and have at least £2,000 in my account.[169]

In January 2012 I moved into my new place, a two-bedroomed council house in Blackley. I had managed to save some money, but it still wasn't enough. I had help from friends and from church to buy the plane ticket for Lynna.

I went to the solicitor again to take all my wage slips and documents, but I also needed a passport before Lynna could come. My passport had been held by the Home Office, and they hadn't returned it. By the time they did, it had expired, so I needed a new one. First of all I went to the police, because I thought my passport had been lost; they gave me a letter for the Zimbabwean embassy. But then the Home Office sent me my old passport, and I was able to fill in the forms from the embassy. I had a paper ID, but it needed to be transferred into a proper passport.

I went to Liverpool with all the documents I needed, and had to pay £600 to have the No Time Limit (NTL) Visa put into my passport. They told me they would ring or write within three working days if it had been approved. They rang me and told me it had gone through, and I could come and pick up the passport. As soon as I got that, I went straight back to the solicitor with my friend Marijke[170] from church, and took all my documents and wage slips. I had just got a wage rise, so that meant I was now earning enough. I also had £2,500 in savings. We submitted everything on 11th March. I had been praying and fasting, and believed that Lynna would come in April. Marijke told me that I needed to be realistic, and the solicitor told me that it might take up to a year, but I had a lot of faith that the visa would come through.

They came and checked the house, and they passed that. Then I had to write a letter to explain why I wanted Lynna to come, and we sent that along with a letter from the landlord to say that I was paying my rent and everything else to Zimbabwe, and left everything in God's hands.

There is no British embassy in Zimbabwe now, just the British consul, so we had to go online to the British embassy in South Africa to see how the case was progressing. I remember trying to log in, but I couldn't do it: it was saying the system was no longer in place, so I rang the Home Office to see what was going on, and they told me they had changed the system. I was devastated that it had happened just when I had applied, and was crying, but the lady on the phone said, 'Why don't you tell your daughter to go to the British consul in Harare and ask?' She went there with the reference number to check and found out that the visa had been granted a week before!

The church had helped to raised £1,000 to cover expenses such as the plane ticket, and Marijke let me use her credit card, because I didn't have one. Then we arranged for Lynna to come.

When we went to register Lynna with the GP, she had to do blood tests, and that's when they discovered that she was pregnant. She didn't know until then. I was shocked; I was heartbroken. After everything I had gone through to bring her here, it had all fallen apart. It wasn't what I wanted for her. I thought that Lynna coming here would at least give me peace of mind, but then when I discovered she was pregnant, it seemed like she had put a knife in my back. I had been doing everything for her, and I felt that I had missed out on things I could have been doing for myself.

Going to work was an escape. I was working 60 hours a week, and because of that I had really been missing out on bonding with Lynna, and also missing out on Tallia when she was born. I was holding on to the anger and pain, and work was my escape. Coming home and seeing Lynna brought back the pain and resentment, and reminded me of what had happened to me back in my youth. It took me almost six months before I could accept the pregnancy. I had really fallen from God's grace, and had to forgive her and forgive myself. It was like everything was dark, and it had come between us and stopped us from bonding.

Things changed when I started to pray and ask God to take away the anger. Then I began to remember how my sister had been there for me when I was pregnant. If she had not been there for me, I would never have had Lynna, and now I would not have become a grandmother. Marijke came in as a mediator between me and Lynna. She had been trying to get into my bubble for almost two years, and never gave up probing until she got in! She was a godsend really.

It was a struggle, but my relationship with Lynna is natural now. We might have a bit of friction here and there, but it's much better than it was when she first came. Back

181

then she saw me more like a friend than a mother, and didn't really have that much respect for me. She had gone through a lot herself, and felt that I had abandoned her, so Marijke was there as a neutral person, not taking sides. Lynna needed to tell me how she felt when my sister died and I wasn't there, and I had to tell her that although I hadn't been able to be there for her physically, I had always been there for her financially and spiritually. And she needed to know what I had gone through too. Whenever I saw other people with their children, I thought, 'That could have been me and Lynna,' and if I saw a young black girl in a uniform, I would think, 'That could have been my Lynna coming home from school.' It was so hard to see mothers holding hands with their children. I didn't even want to go to people's houses from church if they had children.

I finished at the casino on 15th April 2015. I had been there for nearly five years. I had been pastry chef for a long time, but had got tired of that. Then I was on larder (that's starters) for a while; then the head chef had seen my potential and moved me to garnish (that's vegetables). I felt I needed a change in order to progress. I have always aimed high and pushed myself, so I felt it was time to move on. I didn't have a job to go to, so it was a leap of faith.

I went looking for jobs, and had job interviews, but got nothing, so I registered with an agency and got a permanent job on 21st May working just on Saturdays and Sundays. Then I found my current job on 24th July. I am working for the Corsa Club, a new restaurant in Manchester, as a chef doing pastry, and mains sometimes. I have learned what I wanted to learn, and I can see myself, if it's in God's plan, having my own business in five years' time, or being a head chef somewhere. To do that I need a lot of exposure, and need to move on from here, because this is a pub restaurant, and I want to be working in fine dining. I have had two interviews and am waiting to hear about those. I hope to have a new job by the New Year.

I would love to go back to Zimbabwe. I know that things are not like they were when I grew up; it's really different now. But I would love to go back. It would be nice to go back and see where my mum is resting, where my family are resting. I was never able to go to their funerals, so it would be nice just to go and see where they are. I know it will happen one day.

When I went on my first holiday to Egypt, after I got my status, I phoned Immigration to ask if I was really allowed to travel now, and the guy on the phone was laughing and saying, 'Bless you! Yes, you are free; you can travel and go on holiday!'

I said, 'Are you sure? Will I be able to come back?'

He told me, 'Listen, I will give you my name and number, and when you get back to the airport you can ring me!'

I know I could go as far as South Africa or a neighbouring country, but up to now I have been afraid of going anywhere near Zimbabwe. Maybe if Mugabe dies... Honestly, I would love to go back home and help to rebuild the country, maybe not to where it once was, because now it's really down on its knees, but it would be nice just to step on the land again.

Healing for the soul

As everyone who knows Kundai will tell you, she is a very emotional lady. It is not easy for her to hide her emotions, and as she told her story the tears flowed as memories, good and bad, flooded back. We got through a lot of tissues in the two hours 40 minutes that it took to tell!

Kundai is the first to admit that she has not always made the best choices in life. She is very honest about her mistakes, her fears, her frailties, her feelings of guilt. Things that have been done cannot be undone, but her story is one of redemption, restoration and reconciliation. It was not so long ago that she sat in Victoria station that Friday night, not knowing where to go or what to do, fearful of the future and bruised from the battering that life had given her.

Yet the decision to leave the situation she had been in and bravely launch into the unknown was ultimately the turning point of her life, as she put her life firmly in God's hands. Once she had stopped trusting in herself, God could begin the work of soul healing that He specialises in. 'A bruised reed he will not break, and a smouldering wick he will not snuff out. In faithfulness he will bring forth justice,' wrote the prophet Isaiah of the coming Christ.[171]

Now Kundai is beginning to see why she had to go through the things she did: so she can use those experiences for the benefit of others. Nothing is wasted, even the bad things of life, if we give them to God. Working, contributing to society, reconciled with her daughter – Kundai's story, though not complete by any means, is a great inspiration to others living in despair, and a testimony that hope is *never* lost, and that *nothing* is beyond redemption.

---

[156] 'Ian Douglas Smith (1919–2007) was a politician, farmer and fighter pilot who served as prime minister of Rhodesia (or Southern Rhodesia) from 1964 to 1979. His country's first native-born premier, he led the predominantly white government that unilaterally declared independence from the United Kingdom in 1965.'
(https://en.wikipedia.org/wiki/Ian_Smith (accessed 24th March 2016).
[157] 'Robert Mugabe (born 1924) is the current president of Zimbabwe, serving since 22 December 1987. As one of the leaders of the rebel groups against white minority rule, he was elected as prime minister in 1980, and served in that office until 1987, when he became the country's first executive head of state. He has led the Zimbabwe African National Union – Patriotic Front (ZANU–PF) since 1975'
(https://en.wikipedia.org/wiki/Robert_Mugabe (accessed 24th March 2016)).
[158] Up until 1980, 70 per cent of Zimbabwe's land was owned by white farmers, who made up just one per cent of the population. Mugabe set about a programme of land redistribution. The Lancaster House Agreement sought to concede equitable redistribution to the landless without damaging the white farmers' vital contribution to Zimbabwe's economy. After independence in 1980 the reforms began; 'as long as land was sold willingly, the British government would finance half the cost. In the late 1990s, Prime Minister Tony Blair terminated this arrangement when funds available from Margaret Thatcher's administration were exhausted, repudiating all commitments to land reform. Zimbabwe responded by embarking on a "fast track" redistribution campaign, forcibly confiscating white farms without compensation.'
(https://en.wikipedia.org/wiki/Land_reform_in_Zimbabwe (accessed 24th March 2016)
By 2013, every white-owned farm in Zimbabwe had been either expropriated or confirmed for redistribution.

[159] 'The Zimbabwe African People's Union (ZAPU) is a Zimbabwean political party. It was a militant organisation that fought for the national liberation of Zimbabwe from its founding in 1961 until independence in 1980. In 1987 it merged with the Zimbabwe African National Union – Patriotic Front (ZANU - PF) and was relaunched in 2008.'
(https://en.wikipedia.org/wiki/Zimbabwe_African_People%27s_Union (accessed 24th March 2016))

[160] The Movement for Democratic Change was formed in 1999 as the major opposition party to ZANU-PF. It was led by Morgan Tsvangirai, a trade union leader. In 2005 the party split into two factions because of a disagreement emanating from whether it would participate in that year's Senatorial elections. The bigger faction, led by Morgan Tsvangirai, was called MDC-T. The party was part of the Zimbabwe's Government of National Unity between 2008 and 2013 after the disputed 2008 elections, during which there was widespread violence against MDC supporters.

[161] Kundai named the firm, and also gave her solicitor's name. She is not the only person I know to have serious complaints against this firm. Unfortunately there is a 12-month time limit during which a complaint can be made to the SRA, and few asylum seekers are aware of it.

[162] 'Caught' is the word asylum seekers use instead of 'detained'.

[163] It is only a crime if the asylum seeker is not reporting as requested at a Reporting Centre. In that case he could have been accused of harbouring an absconder.

[164] As in Maron's story, Kundai had established a family life in the UK by being together with Marvin for so long. However, being married to a British citizen would not automatically give her the right to stay in the UK, whereas, bizarrely, marrying a citizen from another EU country would. British Law does not confer the right of a spouse from a non-EU country to live here. European Law does.

[165] Asylum Support Housing Advice (ASHA) was set up in October 2004 by Tony Openshaw who had previously worked for the National Coalition for Anti-Deportation Campaigns. The word 'ASHA' means 'hope' in Urdu and 'life' in Swahili. ASHA respects all lives and promotes compassion and understanding to those fleeing persecution and violence. The charity's central aims are to provide support,

advocacy and advice for asylum seekers whose applications have been refused and fully determined, and whose status renders them homeless and destitute. In June 2015 ASHA became a part of the Greater Manchester Immigration Aid Unit when Tony Openshaw retired. (http://www.ashamanchester.wordpress.com (accessed 24th March 2016))

[166] See footnote 49.

[167] As the Boaz Trust developed, so did the programme of well-being and activities, which became known as *Boaz Life*. When Ros Holland became chief executive, she introduced the strapline 'Life in all its Fullness'. This is a reference to Jesus' statement in John's Gospel: 'The thief comes only to steal and kill and destroy; I have come that they may have life, and have it to the full' (John 10:10). This is what we aspire to help our clients realise, despite their circumstances.

[168] The Legacy programme was set up to deal with a vast backlog of asylum applications made before 5th March 2007 which had not been disposed of. Responsibility for dealing with such cases was transferred to the Casework Resolution Directive (CRD). Many of those were liable to removal, having previously exhausted their appeal rights. In 2011 the remaining cases were transferred to the CAAU (Case Assurance Audit Unit). As of 31st March 2013 there were 40,118 unresolved cases. Exactly how many are still undetermined is unclear.

[169] £18,000 a year may not seem much of a wage, but if you have been out of work for years, with nothing on your CV as you seek asylum, it is virtually impossible to find a job paying that much in the first year or two after getting refugee status, much less save up £2,000, at the same time finding and furnishing a place to live so your loved ones can come over. If there are no supportive friends such as Kundai had, families often remain separated for years.

[170] Marijke Hoek, a member of South Manchester Family Church, supporter of the Boaz Trust and a great help and friend to many of the asylum seekers and refugees in the church.

[171] Isaiah 42:3.

Rep's* story

Introduction to Rep's story

This story is different from the six that have gone before, inasmuch as it does not have, as yet, a happy ending. Indeed, it is difficult to see how, naturally speaking, there can be a happy ending, though that could equally have been said of the six previous stories. Someone had other ideas about them! Rep has not been granted sanctuary in the UK, despite having lived here for more than 11 years. Rep is not his real name. I have called him Rep because he is representative of the thousands of genuine refugees who, every year, are refused asylum in the UK, and who are left here in destitution.

The story is also different because it has an international dimension. He came through several other countries before ending up in the UK. He claimed asylum in some of them, so there is, to a certain extent, opportunity for comparison with other systems.

By his own admission Rep lied to authorities, including those in the UK. He regrets doing so now. No one told him how the asylum system works here, and no one advised him well when he needed it, when he first arrived on our shores. Once a mistake has been made in the UK system, even something as small as a wrong date, it is difficult to correct. Ironically, if he had told the simple truth, he may well have been granted asylum, because he ticks all the boxes of what constitutes a genuine refugee. The difficulty, as for the other thousands of so-called 'failed' asylum seekers, is in proving it to a regime that seemingly doesn't want to believe it.

Rep's story takes the lid off what goes on in the UK's black economy, where unscrupulous bosses callously rip off the most vulnerable to line their own pockets. Whatever you think about illegal work, Rep is one of the most hard-working and determined people you could ever meet. I suspect that the majority of people would have turned to *real* crime or simply given up if they had been in his shoes. If everyone in the UK was like him, we would have been much less likely to have gone through a recession. We need more people like him, not less.

Rep's life is still very precarious. Detention and deportation are still real possibilities. He is still, as he has always done, reporting faithfully to Dallas Court, as he is required to do.

For his protection I have given him, his ex-wife, his new wife and some of his closest friends, false names. I have also missed out some dates and place names that might lead to identification.

Rep's story

I was born in the city of Port Sudan, Sudan's second city, in 1980. I have six sisters and five brothers. Along with my twin sister, we are one from last – we just have one younger sister. Because my dad was a teacher I could go to school earlier than most children, at age five. My dad was a maths teacher: that's why I'm good at maths, and my sister has a PhD in maths! I enjoyed school a lot at the beginning. Education was always important for our family.

The area where we lived was very close to the main area inhabited by our tribe, the Beja.[172] Beja is the main name, but under that there are other tribes as well. My dad could speak the Beja language, Bedawi, but didn't want us to speak it. In the villages people spoke Bedawi, but in the town everyone spoke Arabic, and that's what we spoke at home. I just know a few words of Bedawi.

In Port Sudan all the good jobs for young people were in the port, though job opportunities would depend on your family, and if you knew someone working in the port. If you did, it was easy to get a job. They didn't have computer systems like here, so the jobs weren't difficult. Ships were coming in and out all the time, and there were jobs counting the things coming on and off. I was eight years old when I got my first job there in the school holidays.

Although the area was mainly where the Beja lived, the government were always taking people from the provinces and mixing them in the cities. The people with the power came from other places, because the port was very rich, yet there was no good healthcare, education or electricity in the villages because the government looks down on the Beja people.

A lot of people used to come to my dad because he was the teacher and because he was well known, to ask him to go and help with education in other places. However, my dad knew that he could lose his job if he was seen to be too active in the community, and he needed it to feed the family. He was involved in meetings of the Beja congress, but not openly. The government didn't bother, as long as he didn't start a movement or anything like that.

In Sudanese schools it's not like in England. Students have to pay for the books. At the end of the year, if the book is damaged, you don't get your money back. If it's still good and clean, then you carry the money over to the next year, and then you don't have to pay again for the next book. At first you study Islam, Arabic and maths, and then you do more subjects like geography and history as you go along, and you need to pay for those books too. My dad used to secretly keep some of the books and sent them to the small schools in the villages, where they didn't have many.

In Sudan every area has a social club. People go there to play cards or dominoes, watch TV or hold meetings about social and community things. People start going there after six o'clock in the evening, and in the holidays they stay till late. In the port the club was called Al-Nisr. There was no age limit, so we used to go there to play cards and watch TV. The port officers used to be nice to my dad when they were on their own, but not when other people were around. They just wanted to keep their jobs.

Then, when I was about 12, there was a strike against the government. Many people in the port were getting sacked, but it wasn't fair. The company said it needed to cut some jobs, and it was the Beja who were being sacked. Ninety per cent of the Beja were just workers – they didn't have the higher jobs – but even the Beja who were working in the offices, and who had been there a long time, were being kicked out on to the street. And when they kick you out, you don't have any right to complain about how long you have been working there. When your work stops, it stops.

I went on the demonstration with the strikers. I didn't really have any awareness of political things, but people were going, so I went too. After that, things weren't so good with my teachers at school. I got banned from school for a year, and my dad had trouble in his school too. When I was 15 he went to Yemen, because he got a private contract to teach there. He used to send money back; that was a help for us, but my mum started to work too when he left. She got a job in the market. My brothers were all working too, but life was hard, very hard at that time.

My cousin was like a brother to me, more than a brother. He grew up in our house, and we were almost the same age. When I was about 14 he joined the special security forces, just to be on the safe side, and also to give his family some money; the salary is high, even higher than a doctor. Many people from the Beja joined, just to protect themselves. Being an officer in the security forces meant you would have a special ID card and could go anywhere: hospital was free, and you could go to important places. Sometimes you didn't have to pay for things: you just said, 'I'm security.' What happened after this was the main reason I left the country…

When he finished his training they moved my cousin to the capital, Khartoum. His older brother was also in Khartoum, studying chemistry at the university. He was very, very smart – a genius. He fell in love with a girl there. She asked him to help her after uni with her chemistry, and she invited him to her home. So he went back with her to study. He didn't know that her dad was an officer in the security forces. They were sitting in her dad's office to study. Normally she would have studied in the other room, but her mum had visitors. It's traditional that when you have visitors you bring them juice or tea or something, so she went out to help her mum. When she had gone, my cousin started to read the titles of all the files. He found a government file about the war, and started reading it.

At that time there was still a war in South Sudan. This file was about officers in the government forces, who they knew were going to make trouble. They knew they had some information and felt like they were going to do something against the government. They weren't going to put them on trial in the capital or anything – they would just send them to the front line in South Sudan or Darfur, and someone would shoot them there.

My older cousin took the file and hid it, but the girl's dad knew it was him who had taken it. He went to look for him at the uni, but didn't find him. My cousin ran away. He was hoping to find a journalist to give the file to. His friends advised him to go back to his own area and hide there, because it was too dangerous in the capital. There are many villages between Port Sudan and Kassala[173] where he could hide. It was either that or leave the country, so he went on the camel way to Egypt, but the Egyptian security forces caught him and sent him back to the government in Khartoum, where they killed him.[174]

At that time I was staying with my cousin in Khartoum, who was trying to find out what had happened to his older brother. The security forces brought his body and said that he had hanged himself in his room. They said he had hanged himself from the fan on the ceiling, but the fan wasn't strong enough to hang an adult body.

After the funeral my cousin started to ask around why they had killed him. When he did that the security forces thought *he* was going to start something, so they interviewed him. He knew about the file – he had told me about that. Normally I would meet him after work, but one day I had gone to meet some relatives of my dad, and when I got back I got a phone call from his family back home. A doctor had called them to tell them that my cousin had hanged himself. He had said that he had had psychological problems after his brother had died, and his mind didn't accept it, but I *know* he wasn't going to hang himself.

I went to the hospital to see the body, but at first they didn't let me. Later when I saw the body, I could see the mark from the rope around his neck. It was a horrible thing to see. I travelled back to Port Sudan with the body in the back of a pick-up. It's a long journey, about 18 hours.

After we had buried him, the officers started to watch me too, and to ask about me, because I had been with my cousin for about six weeks.

I talked to my oldest brother, who is a teacher too. He told me to just keep quiet and continue my life as normal because up to then things had been OK. He said, 'Don't even try to ask about anything, and don't go anywhere. Don't try to do *anything*.' I stayed with his family and my family, and kept on studying. Then they sent for me. My brother went with me the first time, but they didn't let him in. The officer asked me about myself and my two cousins, and told me not to leave the city. I also had to report to them every 24 hours. I just had to come and show my face, and then I could go. They said they might interview me again at any time. They said, 'We don't want to detain you now. As long as you go along with us, we will be nice to you. We don't want you to lose your future.'

I went back with my brother and explained everything to him. At that time my dad had come back from Yemen. He had used the money from teaching in Yemen to buy a Toyota pick-up. He put a roof on it and seats inside, and turned it into a type of taxi for 12 people – plus two in the front. He used to drive people around town. My brother advised me not to tell my dad, in case they interviewed him and he knew.

For a few days everything went fine. I reported every day, and my brother went with me and waited far away from the office for me to come out. Sometimes I was there for two, three, four hours with no food, and then they would let me go. It just depended on the officer who was there: if he was nice it would be one or two hours, but sometimes it was six hours. They don't talk to you. They just tell you when you can go. Sometimes they ask you about the same things as before, and then let you go.

I started to get nervous because I knew the interview was coming. I didn't know when it was going to be, or what it was going to be like. I started to get scared, so I didn't go. On the first day nothing happened, so I thought they were just playing with me. My brother told me it was better to keep going because as long as you are going they don't bother you, but I said I wasn't going to go, and that if anything happened I was going to tell my dad. He said, and I still remember it now, 'You are going to bring trouble on your dad and brother and sister.'

So I said, 'Then I am not going to stay in the house.'

I went to stay with a friend who lived near the edge of the city. Then my sister came and told me they had been looking for me, and they had taken my dad, so I went to Kassala.[175] From there I contacted my family by phone, and found out my dad had been arrested. They had also taken his Toyota taxi-car. My mum told me to stay away. She knew – everyone now knew the story.

My oldest brother met my dad before they took him to the capital. My dad told him to tell me to go to someone in Kassala who would sort things for me. The man knew my dad very well. He told me to leave the country. It was almost Christmas time, and the city was busy at that time, because there are a lot of celebrations between Christmas and New Year. I came back to see my family, and then I left on the train for Egypt. I was nearly 16.

I took my brother's passport, because he was not on the wanted list, so he was able to get a visa. I don't really look like my brother, but from my experience people don't really check the picture. They care more about whether the passport is real. Also, there was no system for scanning.

You know what I was most scared about? It wasn't the Egyptian security when I reached Aswan in Egypt; it was being caught by an officer on the train. The train took the whole day. They could have come at any time. Whenever the train stopped, I got out, and got back in when the train was going to leave, and I kept changing seats. It was the most horrible journey in my whole life. At the time I didn't think about missing my mum or family, or what was going to happen to my dad, or that I had just 13 dollars in my pocket, or what I was going to eat: I just cared about whether they were going to catch me.

When the train got to Halfa we went on a ship overnight to Aswan. The security there was less of a headache than on the train.

I didn't know anyone in Egypt, and I didn't know where to go; there are 80 or 90 million people. I wasn't even 16, and I had to survive with 13 dollars in my pocket! I didn't even know where I could go to change it. I went to a lot of places to try and get a falafel sandwich, but they didn't accept dollars. They all told me to go and change my money. One guy who was selling sandwiches on the street with his wife was really nice. He told me not to show dollars to people on the street, because that could get me killed. They showed me the place to change the money, but I was scared to go, because I didn't know what to do. But the hotel accepted it. I stayed there one night. When I went to get a ticket for Cairo, the money wasn't enough, so I had to stay in Aswan.

Someone told me about a Sudanese guy who was working in the other hotel. I met him and explained the situation. He said, 'Go up on top of the train, then you won't have to pay, or stay in the toilet when the control comes.' I thought it was safer to stay in the toilet, as I have a problem with heights – they make me feel dizzy. So I hid in the toilet when the man came. When he banged on the toilet, I just stayed there till he went away. Once he stopped me and asked for the ticket. I told him it was with my dad, and he was at the end of the train. I said I was just fetching something, then going back to my seat.

When I got to Cairo I had about four dollars in my pocket. I had no idea where to go. I found a shisha place and asked for tea. I asked the guy where I could change the money, and he said he would give me a better price, so I gave him two dollars. He told me there was a Sudanese guy working for a big Egyptian family nearby, so I went to see him. He was a really nice guy from the North. I lied to him, to be honest, just to make him feel like I needed help. I told him I had come to Egypt to study, and they had stolen my money on the train. I didn't tell him the truth, just to protect myself. I told him I couldn't go back to my family and that I needed to work, so he let me stay with him.

He was working in the family store, working with chemicals used in batteries, and chlorine and zinc. I used to go with the driver to bring it back to the store. I burned my arm on some of the chemicals, and still have a big scar. There weren't any health and safety regulations, and I was paid about 50 Egyptian pounds a week, working six days. I survived on that because I didn't have many expenses.

On Sunday we went to Abbassia, a district of Cairo, where there was a big church. A friend told me about the United Nations programme there. He had been accepted as a refugee. I slept in the street and went there next morning, and they gave me an appointment, but I didn't tell them my story because I was scared they were going to send me back.

From there I went with that friend to a village called Tarabin near Nuweiba Beach in Sinai. He told me it was lot freer round there. We used to sleep on the beach. I soon got a job in a restaurant, because I had studied and learned English and Hebrew very quickly. Then they put me to work in the supermarket selling things to tourists. After a while they put me in charge of organising the whole supermarket for the village. They called it the Blue Bus camp, because there was the shell of a blue bus there, which had come there and broken down. I got really good money. There were lots of tourists, and I used to look after the tourists' passports, money and jewellery while they were in the village. I was really honest, and often they would give me money when they left.

After I had been in Egypt for about a year and a half there was a problem between Israel and Palestine, and the tourism stopped. They started to lay off people in the restaurant, but they kept me because I was working in the restaurant and also working outside as a waiter, and also because I had been honest and had made no problems for them. Then things got worse and worse, and they started selling the restaurant. So I decided to get all my money and send it to my family in Sudan.

While I was there I had made some good contacts with people from Sudan, and one of the guys advised me to go to Syria, because I didn't need a visa for that. Then I could go to Turkey from there. So I went to Syria with the same passport, my brother's. In Syria I got a visa for Turkey, and went there.

Then I paid someone 600 dollars to get me to Europe. They put us on an inflatable boat, and although we kept saying it was full, they kept bringing people. There were 45 of us on an inflatable boat going to Greece. Then they asked, 'Who knows how to drive?' Someone said they did, and they put him at the back to steer. They told us it would take two hours, then we would be safe, but they lied to us. We set off early morning, and it was almost dark when we were stopped by the Greek navy. It was so packed that you couldn't move. If you wanted to pee you just had to do it down your leg. The officer told us that we could not enter Greece. They were nice to us, actually. They gave us some food and filled up the engine with petrol; then they sent us back to Turkey. When we got back, the police caught us and interviewed us. Then they left us alone.

After that I found someone who said he could sort out a safe way for me to get to Europe. He said I needed to pay him, so I told him I didn't have much money. If I had told him how much I had, he would have taken it all. That's what they do. With my passport he got me a ticket on KLM. My ticket was first for Amsterdam, then to Egypt, then on another airline to Sudan. That made it look like I was going back home, but he told me to ask for asylum when I got to Amsterdam. I never knew, when I left my country, that you have the right to ask for asylum in another country. Back then we weren't aware of this. People understand more now because of the media, but back then no one knew.

He told me that if I knew anyone in Holland I should send my passport in the post to them when I got to the airport in Amsterdam, because no one would check the post – and if I didn't know anyone, I should tear it up and put it down the toilet on the plane. So that's what I did: I destroyed the passport, and when I got to Amsterdam, I asked for asylum.

Holland was a big headache, honestly. At that time they decided that anyone from North Sudan didn't have a problem. They gave asylum to people from South Sudan, Darfur or the Nuba Mountains, but not from the North. There was nothing in the media about trouble there, so they thought there was no problem. There are so many dirty things being done by the government in Sudan,[176] but they just don't get into the media. But if you said you were from Darfur, they would accept you – even if you were Egyptian! It was hard to understand the whole system: you needed to lie. I was scared that they would find out about me from the aeroplane list, so I changed my name. That's what my friends told me to do. I didn't have awareness at that time that a country like Holland would protect you if you had a problem.

Sudan is like a closed country. You have two choices: if you want a nice life, forget about what you have been taught about being good – follow the government, go with the corruption, shut your mouth. You will have good money and a nice life. Or, on the other hand, you can die. It's like a game of chess – fly or die. You don't have another option. If you want to go straight, you are going to die. If you go with the government, you fly – that's exactly how it is.

I was in Holland for nearly two years. I was in an old military camp in the South with a lot of Kurdish Iraqis and African asylum seekers in it. Then they sent me to a camp in the North, which was in the middle of nowhere. I worked illegally, delivering newspapers. I used to get up at three in the morning, go to the office, deliver the newspapers, go to the station at six o'clock, buy a ticket and go to report every week.

My life was alright when I was working in Holland, but not in the asylum system. There is more freedom and there are more rights in England. In Holland you are not allowed to choose your solicitor. They give you a solicitor, and it's like the solicitor is interviewing you as well as the IND.[177] You don't know anything, and the language is a big problem. There is nothing to do in the camp, just sitting there all day, and people used to end up doing drugs, which you can find anywhere in Holland. It's also difficult to make friends with Dutch people, not like in England, where you are in a house in the asylum system, and you don't feel so different to other people. I only made friends with one family in Holland, the family of a journalist that I had met in the village in Sinai.

I left the camp and went to Germany to work, because there is no border. I worked in McDonald's! I also went to do building work in France in the summer, for an Arab who built a big house in the forest. I had an ID card from Holland, but it was useless. You can't do anything with it. I wanted to get a scooter so I could deliver the papers, but they wouldn't give me a licence because I was under 24. I had to pass a CBR[178] exam to get my licence, so I studied hard and watched a DVD of how to do the exam for about five weeks, and even though it was in a different language, I passed! In Haarlem I delivered about 400 papers every morning, and never made a mistake. I never missed an address or delivered the wrong paper.

I felt that my file was going to be closed in Holland, so I went to seek asylum in Sweden with a Somalian ID. It was an original, not a fake. I got it in Den Haag. There's a guy there – you pay him 1,000 euros and he will find your twin on a passport. It looked just like me. When I was in Sweden I lied and told them I was from Nuba, but they didn't accept it. They told me that Sudanese cases weren't working, and that I would be waiting for nothing. I just wanted to get somewhere where I didn't have to work in the black economy. Even in Holland I had to pay my wages into someone else's account, and then they would take some of it. But you can't say anything – you just have to shut your mouth.

I was in Sweden for about six weeks; then I was planning to fly to Canada. They told me about a guy in Den Bosch who would help me. I went to meet him, and we talked, but he was asking too much – 3,000 euros. So I went back to work so I could earn more money. I didn't have any other option. Then my asylum file was closed and they asked me to leave.

To get more time in Holland, I told them I was going to go back home voluntarily. That gave me another two or three months legally in the country. I was planning to go to Canada, to be honest, and was going to save up the money in those three months. One guy scared me, though. He told me that if your time is finished in the country, and they stop you, and you are illegal, they would deport you. That scared me a lot.

Then I was advised to go to the UK. Because it was before 2003, they hadn't taken my fingerprints, so I could go and claim asylum anywhere in Europe.[179]

At that time my mum needed an operation, so it was very hard: I had to either use the money to send to my mum, or use it to survive myself. I talked to my brother and sister, and they told me to sort myself out and they would try to do something for my mum.

The first time I tried to get to the UK, I was on a Euroline bus, but security checked the bus in France, and they saw it wasn't my ID. They took me to an office to interview me, and the interpreter said that they were offering for me to claim asylum there in France, but from the information that I had the French didn't care, and they could leave you there with nothing for many years. You were not allowed to do anything, so I told the French that I didn't want asylum there; I was asking for it in the Netherlands. I showed them my Dutch ID card, and they finished the interview – but I didn't get my Somalian passport back.

I went back to Holland, and I had no money. I had lost everything. I just had 18 euros left. I knew a friend from the camp, who I had helped before to find a job with the newspaper. He had a girlfriend from Dominica who had Dutch nationality. They had got married and he went to live with her, but he still had his room in the camp. I stayed in his room, and he lent me the money. We went to a Moroccan guy who wanted 1,600 euros to get me into the UK. My friend gave him 1,000 and said he would get the rest when I had arrived safely. Actually the guy didn't do *anything*. He just put me somewhere for one night: he didn't even bring me food.

We got tickets to go to a port near the border with Belgium, and there was a ship there going to Dover. We went to a takeaway, and he told me that I needed to change all my clothes and get rid of anything that could be identified as coming from Holland.

He showed me the boat. It was a ferry for trucks, not for people. There were two fences to get over. The first one was quite low, and we climbed that. The second one was much higher, about two metres high. I think he had worked here before, because he knew where things were. He told me where the security room was, and how to pass it. Then he told me that there were two lines of trucks: one was going on to the boat, and the other coming off it and going somewhere in Europe. He helped me over the wall, and I went into the line of trucks. I climbed between the wheels of one of the trucks, like he told me. The officer came and checked everything, but he passed by me. Then the lorry went into the ship. You know, it would be very easy to die, because when the truck went into the ship the wheels moved up and down, and the back wheels don't seem to belong to each other. It hurts your bones, and you think you are going to die.

It was February, and I was cold and hungry. I was scared, because I didn't know where the ship was going. Then it started to move. I reached for my Qur'an to protect me. In this situation you just need to feel close to God.

The ship moved all night. It was so cold, and although it wasn't raining, it felt like it was wet. Then the ship stopped, and the trucks began to move one by one. My truck started to move, then stopped. When it stopped, I got down. It was still in the port at Dover, and it was sunrise. Then I was stopped by an officer. I felt sick, but I couldn't throw up. I had a piece of paper with my friend's number on it in Holland. I couldn't remember it, so I had written it down. I put it in my mouth, in case anything went wrong, and I needed to get rid of it.

Rep's Journey

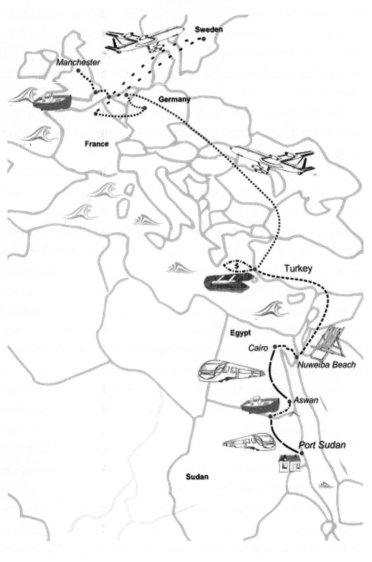

The officers were really nice. They took me to a room and said they had to check everything on me. They could see I was sick and shaking from the cold. I said that I needed to go to the toilet, so they took me there. While I was there I took the paper out of my mouth and put it down the toilet, because it was evidence of where I had come from.

They took me to the interview. There was a lady officer and a Kurdish interpreter. He had six fingers: I will never forget it in my life!

They were horrible to me. The lady didn't say anything. It was the interpreter who did the interviewing! He said, 'We will send you back to your country. We know you are lying.' He kept saying it. When he asked me about my family, I told him about my father, mother, brother and sister. At that point he said, 'Stop. We don't need the names of the whole village.' That's why the Home Office don't know anything about my sisters and brothers. I wanted to tell them, but he stopped me. Anyway, the interview just went horribly. I had a big, long coat full of oil, and my clothes already smelled, because I had gone two days without a shower. The only information I had given them was my name, date of birth, my country and how I came to the UK. I lied about that. I said I had come by ship from Port Sudan, but the interpreter said he believed I had just got on the ship in England to make it look like I had come from abroad. He was really horrible.

When the interview was over, they gave me the Home Office card. At the time I thought that meant that I was going to be accepted. After that they sent me to the hostel, where I met some Sudanese and started to make some friends. When we discussed my situation, they told me that I needed to say either that I was from Darfur or that I was Beja but had been involved in the war. I wrote down a story that I had been involved in the war, had been in detention, escaped and run away. They said that story would be stronger, but now I know my real case is stronger than this story. It's just that is what people want you to say, so you have to say it. Then I destroyed the paper with my story on, in case anyone found it.

Most asylum seekers have the wrong information. While you are in the hostel, they scare you about many things. They said, 'Tell them you don't speak English. Tell them you haven't been to school and don't know how to read and write. If you do that, they will accept you.' Some of the people who did that had finished uni! But because you don't know anything about anything, and these are people from your country, you listen to them. Nobody tells you anything about the asylum system, about how it works. There is no information at all.

So they gave me my first interview[180] in London. I didn't know where it was or how to get there. An Albanian guy showed me where the buses stopped and said, 'You speak English: just keep asking.' Although I had already got a solicitor, I hadn't met him, and he didn't come.

At the interview they were really nice, and I honestly felt stupid and really bad that I had lied to them. It lasted about two hours. You know what the worst thing is, the thing that really hurts you? When you lie at the beginning, it follows you all your life. This is the problem. But the good thing is, I didn't lie about my name. I just felt I had to tell some of the truth.

When I returned to the hostel I saw my name up on the board. I was being transferred to Rochdale. I had only been in the hostel five days. That was quick: some people stay much longer, up to a month.

I had no idea where Rochdale was. When I got there, the manager of the accommodation was really nice. When I went to the office he gave me a warm, waterproof jacket. I really appreciated that, because I didn't have money to buy clothes. After that I started to get my asylum money from the post office.

After two weeks I got an appointment with my solicitor. He told me that he had a copy of my initial interview, but not my screening interview. He said he would write to the Home Office to get a copy, but he never got one, and until today I have never seen a copy of my screening interview. I complained to him about the interpreter. When I said he had six fingers, he knew straight away who I was talking about, and said they had received so many complaints about him. Some people thought he was working for the Home Office.

The Home Office made a mistake. They got the day I came to the UK wrong. They still use the wrong date, even today.[181]

Shortly afterwards I got refused. It was in March 2005. I hadn't been in the house very long. I didn't get a letter from the Home Office. I got a letter to say that I had to leave the house because my file was closed. I rang the solicitor, and he told me to fax the letter over to him. I did that, and he contacted them. They said a decision had been made, and there had been no appeal. My solicitor told them that he had received nothing from the Home Office, and neither

209

had I. They called NASS[182] back, and put me back in the system. After that I received the decision. My money had been stopped for about two weeks.

I went to see the solicitor again to prepare for court. He told me he would not be going, but a barrister would be there. I took a witness with me to court. He was a member of the Beja Congress[183] here in the UK. He knew me, and he knew my dad, but the judge didn't take it into account. I don't know why.

By this time I was already going to college. Rochdale College had told me to come back in September, so I went to 'learndirect'. They had two courses: introductory English and intermediate English. I thought that I would learn English and then maybe do engineering, so I could get a nice job. I wanted to earn a lot of money so I could get my dad out of detention. My family back home couldn't afford it.

While I was waiting for a decision about the course at Rochdale College, in July, I got a refusal from the court. I had five days to appeal. Three days after the decision my solicitor said he was going to send the case to a specialist to see if there were grounds for an appeal – and on the last day he told me there were no grounds.

I went to the NASS office for advice. They told me to go to Citizens Advice. I went there, and they told me to come back the next day. I went to Refugee Action, and they said the same, but I had to do something, so I went to a solicitor's near Rochdale train station. There was a lady solicitor there, I think from Pakistan, who said she would help me to write the appeal, but I would have to send it in myself. She helped me to fill in the application form and write the appeal. I sent it by fax, then sent off the copy in the post. I got a reply to say they had received the appeal, and I would have to wait.

After finishing my language course at college, they transferred me to Bury. I had been in college for a year. Then, when I started the engineering course, I got a refusal of the appeal. I went everywhere looking for a solicitor, but no one would take on my case, so I wrote an appeal to the high court myself, but that was refused too. Then they kicked me out of the house.

I knocked on so many doors, but no one would take me. I understand it wasn't because they didn't want me; it was because of the NASS system. They didn't want to lose their accommodation, and the ones in the Sudanese community who had status were busy with work and just getting on with their lives. You could stay with people for one or two days, but you would have to sleep fully dressed and get up at seven in the morning so that, if anyone came, you could say you had not been sleeping there. From Friday, especially after five, to Sunday or Monday morning, no one would come. You could stay anywhere on the weekend. The problem is, you have to take your bag with you from house to house, and you have no ticket and no money. You can't imagine how many times I walked from Rochdale to Manchester; on the bus it takes an hour. I was still going to Hopwood College in Rochdale. In the first year of engineering they still had my letter from NASS, so I didn't have to pay, but in the second year I had to pay.[184]

That same year, 2007, my dad passed away in detention. He was a really strong man. He wasn't just a teacher; he used to do building work in the holidays. He was really good at building, and he used to do small DIY jobs after work. I couldn't work and couldn't afford to get him out of detention at that time. Everything was closed to me, and I had to leave college. I couldn't carry on.

I came to Manchester to find work, and I was doing a lot of leafleting for takeaways. Sometimes they didn't pay me, but I still had to do the work in the hope that they would pay me. I was still living in Rochdale and would wake up early in the morning and come to Manchester. I would do 1,000 leaflets, then go to the takeaway and ask for some money. Either they would give it to me or they would give me some food and take that from my wages. At that time you would get £20 for 1,000. Sometimes it would take a day and a half to do 1,000. It depended on the area. They didn't care if you got wet: they cared more about the leaflets getting wet. And they watched you, to see if you were delivering or not. Sometimes they wouldn't give you anything until you had delivered 4,000 leaflets – then they would pay you for 1,000 and take the money for the first 3,000 as a deposit, and if they found out you weren't delivering, you wouldn't get your money back. But they never gave you the full amount for what you had done. Leafleting was horrible. Sometimes my feet swelled and were bigger than my shoes.

I used to get some support from some English friends. I met them when I was working at the Blue Bus camp in Egypt. They taught English for the British Council, and used to go there for holidays. We kept in touch, and I met them again when I came to the UK in 2005. Whenever I had a problem I would phone them and they would support me.

After my dad died I was a bit of a mess. I didn't care about my studies; I didn't care about anything. My whole life was a mess. I started to drink a lot: we used to buy two-litre bottles of cheap cider, especially at the weekends. We would make a big meal and then drink until early in the morning, and we would be out of it the whole next day. I spent all my energies in online chat rooms. That's where I met a girl from Brazil* called Maria*, and we started a relationship online.

I was staying with one friend, and I could tell by his eyes that he wanted me to go, but he understood my situation. The housing officers came many times, but I told them I was just a visitor. They said, 'If you are here next time, we know you are staying here.' I told my friend I didn't want to make trouble for him, and I left. At the same time I was getting food and a bus ticket from the church in Old Trafford.[185] That helped a lot. After a while I got a room in a house in Moston with the Boaz Trust. It was helpful just to have a place to stay.

Then I got a job in Gorton, working for three months on 11 flats. There was nothing there when we started, just walls, a roof and wires. The guys I was working with were professionals. I learned how to do plasterboard, skimming, painting – lots of things. For the whole week I would get a maximum of £50, and sometimes they would say that the guy who owned it was in Pakistan. He was a millionaire and had a big hotel in Spain, so I don't know why he couldn't pay.

The guy I was working for had a big DIY store in Old Trafford. We used to go there to pick stuff up for work. It had 10 or 12 flats above it that he rented out to Polish people. When we finished the job, the place where he stored all his stuff burned down, and the insurance company refused to pay because he didn't have CCTV, so he said he couldn't pay us. He said he would later, but I don't think I got more than £300 for three months' work.

After that I worked with another guy in the building trade. At first he paid me, but then he stopped, so I left him, but I didn't complain, because I didn't want any problems with the police.

At the end of 2007 I went to see a solicitor in Birmingham. He asked me to bring some proof from the Beja Congress, so he could make a fresh claim. I didn't have money to go to London to get it from them, so I phoned the leader of the Beja in the UK. One of my British friends went and picked it up for me, and brought it to me. I didn't tell the leader that I had no money, because he knew my family, and I didn't want them to know that I was in a bad situation. I took the evidence to the solicitors, and they lost it in the office – how, I don't know. I phoned the leader again and asked him if he could send it by post this time. He said he wanted to see my face, so I borrowed some money, went to get it and took it to Birmingham.

Then I got a job in Longsight, working with two guys in building. I wanted to learn new things and get experience. It's really easy to get an illegal job in the building trade; the problem is getting paid. They all know each other, and though they can't stand each other, if you have an argument with one of them, none of the others will accept you. If you don't get your money, you just have to walk.

I also worked in a cash and carry. The store closed at eight o'clock, and I used to get there at ten to restock the store. We carried loads of stuff. And I saw so many bad things. They used to take meat from Tesco that had reached its expiry date and reuse it as halal. They would just put it in a new packet with a new sticker on it. That's why I never buy from them. But you can't go to the police. You just keep your mouth shut. I decided to leave, but when I asked for my money they said, 'No, the boss is not here.' That's always the excuse: 'The boss is not here.' I don't know how many hundreds of times I have heard that.

After that I went back to leafleting, because I was working on my own, and at least I would get 50 per cent of the money. And I was honest, not like other people who threw some of them away – I delivered every last leaflet. Sometimes being honest hurts you more.

After that I spoke to a friend in Rochdale who worked in a factory. He told me I could get a job there. I told him that I didn't have a National Insurance number, but he said there was someone in Birmingham who could do it for me. He gave me the number, and I phoned the guy. He told me to come to Birmingham and he would sort it out for me. I took a photo with me, and he gave me a Portuguese ID and a National Insurance number. I paid him £75, which was a lot of money for me at that time. Nowadays it doesn't work – you need an original.

I went to the agency. I was scared, to be honest. They gave me an ID to get money from the bank. They paid by cheque. So I worked in the factory. They paid me really well. I was paid £120 a week for working Saturday and Sunday 6pm to 6am. On Monday morning I would go back to Rochdale, take a shower, change my clothes and go to study. I did that for a year. I was living with a guy; I paid him £35 a week rent, and we shared the food. I really worked hard at the factory, and they respected me. It was a vegetable packing factory. I worked on the line, in dispatch, cleaning – many areas. I used to help the supervisor. Then there was a fire in the factory. They made a small emergency factory from an old storeroom, but there were only two lines there. I was chosen to work there, but after a while the work stopped.

I had saved enough money for two weeks. After that I was back on leaflets and building work. I worked for a while in Sale. The houses there were really nice – you could only dream about them. When the job was finished, they didn't give me all the money – I got almost half of it. So it was back to leaflets. One of the jobs was for a restaurant in the suburbs of Manchester. After leafleting they offered me a job in the restaurant. First I did three weeks' training. I didn't get paid anything for that. I just got free food. I had to borrow money for transport and clothes from Primark.

Then the restaurant opened, and I started work there. They didn't pay good money, but the good thing was that I got breakfast, lunch and dinner there, and I could take home what was left at the end of the night. The other good thing was that they did pay fairly – I worked 12 hours a day for 30 pounds.[186] It was a regular job, and I started to save. I sent some money to my family, and I started to save so that Maria was able to come over from Brazil on a student visa. I worked really hard, six days a week, so I could pay her college fees, which were £5,400 for the first two years.

One day I went to sign at Dallas Court[187] as normal: I had to sign once a month. The room there was full, and someone came in and shouted my name. I went with him, and he told me they were going to ask me about a medical check. When I went in, they asked me if I had any problems, and I told them that I only had Hepatitis B, but the doctor had told me I didn't need to take any medicine: I just needed to go for a blood check every year.

Then they suddenly told me, 'You are under arrest. Your file has been closed.' It was like a knife in my heart. By then I had a new solicitor, a really nice old man called Roger, who had put in a fresh claim for me. The Home Office hadn't responded. The good thing was that they gave me my phone back, so I could call Maria, as well as one of my British supporters, and Boaz, even though I didn't have much battery left.

I don't know if it was related or not, but Maria and I had an appointment to be legally married at the registry office the next week. Before that we had just had an Islamic wedding.

After Dallas Court closed they took me to the detention centre at Manchester Airport. We didn't stay there for long – about four or five hours. Early in the morning, maybe at about three o'clock, they took us to London. I don't remember which centre it was.[188] When we arrived there it was eight o'clock. There were so many people from different countries. I didn't think I was going to be in a place like that. They told me to get something to eat and go back to the office in an hour. I went back at nine, and they put me in a car. I thought they were taking me to another centre or something, because I didn't have anything with me except the clothes I was wearing. They had even taken my mobile.

217

They didn't tell me where we were going, but they took me to the Sudanese embassy, which was a surprise for me. It was the hardest thing ever. I was scared of the embassy, and when the car stopped outside the embassy, they put handcuffs on me. There was a group of Sudanese outside the embassy, waiting for something. They were watching me, and I will never, ever forget how I felt. I wasn't a criminal: they didn't need to put handcuffs on me in front of those people. I wasn't running. I was still in shock from being arrested, and they didn't inform me that we were going to the Sudanese embassy. I thought my mind was going to explode.

In the embassy the interviewer asked me who I was and why I was in England. I told him I was there to study. He asked me if I had a problem back home, and I said, 'No. I am just here to study.' I thought I would play it that way, and then I asked him, 'What are you going to do now?'

'The Home Office are going to ask for a travel document, and we are going to send it to them,' he replied.

I told him, 'I have a wife here. She's not Sudanese – she's Brazilian. I am paying for her studies.'

He said, 'Are you working?'

I said, 'Illegally.'

He looked at me, but he didn't say anything. He just kept writing. He said to the officers, who were sitting on a sofa behind me, 'The interview is finished. He's Sudanese.' They put the handcuffs back on me, and took me back to detention. But this time I didn't care who saw me in handcuffs.

On the way back I talked to the guards. I told them, 'I have been really nice in this country. I haven't done anything wrong. I'm not a criminal. I have never been to the police station. You don't need to put me in these things,' gesturing to my handcuffs, but they didn't answer me.

They took me back, and from then on, every day I thought they would send the travel document and send me back to Sudan. You start hearing stories about how they force people to go back,[189] and that made it worse and worse.

At the same time I was thinking about how my wife was going to survive. All of my attention was on Maria. She was not working, so how was she going to pay for bus fares? How was she going to get food, and how would she manage? The thing is, at that time her visa was running out. She needed to renew it, because she had applied to uni and been accepted, and she also needed to show £15,000 in her bank account for the first year – £8,400 for the course and the rest for living expenses. It had to be in her account for 28 days. I was in detention and could not earn any money. I was really worried. If I had been on my own, I would not have cared.

While I was there, I tried to kill time. I had two jobs. I used to work in the kitchen early in the morning, making and serving breakfast, cleaning the kitchen, then making and serving lunch, and cleaning the kitchen again. Then, at ten o'clock when the doors were closed, I was a cleaner. After two weeks they noticed that I had two jobs, and stopped one of them. I used to get about £2.50 an hour. It wasn't much, but I could buy a few cigarettes. I used to smoke at that time. I also gave some of it to Maria for bus tickets. My British friends also helped a lot. I will never forget this.

I knew all the officers in the centre, and used to play chess with them after breakfast. I got on fine with the guards, but in the main office it was really bad. They treat you like you are a criminal, and at the medical centre as well. One time I had really bad stomach pains and a high fever. Your cell door is locked at ten o'clock, and you are not allowed out after that. There is a bell for emergencies, so I pressed the bell. The warder came. He could see I was sick. He said, 'Are you sick? You're not pretending?'

I said, 'No, I swear I'm not. I'm really sick. I really, really need help.'

He said, 'Have you been smoking drugs or anything?'

'No. I don't smoke drugs,' I told him.

He said, 'OK, I'm going to send for the nurse.'

About an hour later they came back and opened the door. There are two doors – they kept the second one closed. They gave me a drink in a small plastic measuring cup. They didn't ask me what it felt like, or what was wrong. They just said, 'Drink some water and go to sleep. You are going to be fine.' That was it.

The next day it was still the same. I went to the medical centre. They treat you really, really badly – I don't feel like they are human. I went back from the medical centre. I know one guy who works in the removal centre – he's Sudanese. He's there two days a week. I don't know exactly what his job is. I think he advises people about returning to their country. I went to him and told him I was sick and the medical people had done nothing for me. He said he would see what he could do. The next day he came and gave me some medicine, then left. He was allowed to go in and out of the medical centre. That was the only good medicine I got – and it worked!

You do get a proper breakfast, lunch and dinner, but life inside is just crazy. When you are outside, you are safe but you have no food. When you are inside, you have food but you are not safe. I don't know; it was just crazy. I applied for bail, but the Home Office said I might run off, and the judge agreed, but I had only ever missed reporting twice, and that was when my dad died. It was hard for me then, and I wasn't thinking about reporting. I applied for bail seven times, and every time it was refused.[190]

Even though I was in detention, my wife got her visa. Three of our friends put the money in her account. That was a big help.

I was there for three months. Then, one day, I had just finished working in the kitchen. I was lying on my bed, taking a break before having a shower. My wife was visiting me that day. Visiting started after 12 o'clock, and I was getting ready. One of the security staff, an Indian lady, came and asked me, 'What are you doing here?'

I told her, 'I'm sorry, I just came from finishing work in the kitchen and I'm feeling a bit tired. I am just going to go and visit with my wife.'

She said, 'No, you don't need to go and visit her.' I asked her why and she said, 'Because you are going home.' I couldn't believe it. She said, 'You've got one hour to take your stuff, and then I don't want to see you again in this room.' I told Maria to just wait for me outside. She came, and we went home together.[191]

I don't know why they released me. I didn't ask, and they never said. Maybe it was something that Roger[192] did. He was in contact with me while I was in detention.[193]

We arrived home in the early morning. The next day I went to the restaurant, and I was back working again. But from then on relations between me and my wife were not like before. She knew it was not safe. I was stressed, and most of the time we argued. We had so much debt. We owed £1,550 for rent and council tax after three months in detention, and we owed money to friends who had helped. On top of that I was coming home at one or two in the morning, and she was getting up at six to get ready to go to uni. We only had time together on Sunday. We did get married at the registry office as we had planned, but we even argued on the way there. There was so much worry that it reached the point where she couldn't handle the debt, and I couldn't handle it either. She asked me to leave the house, so I did, and even though we tried again for a few days, it didn't work. I was so completely focused on my fresh claim and paying off the debt that I even forgot about my family back home. I used to spend five pounds every week on a phone card to speak to them, but that became every month, and even then I felt there was nothing to say.

My relationship with Maria was fine in the beginning. We had a nice time. It was just the stress of the asylum claim. I don't advise anyone in my situation to have a relationship, because it's bad for the other person too. I was working six days, and on the other day you need to sleep, but you also need to go out with your wife. At the same time you are paying the rent, gas, electricity, transport for your wife – all this stuff. After the divorce I went back to drink, but Gina*[194] was there for me, and I was also seeing a counsellor every week for about a year. Maria came to the counsellor for the first meeting; after that she refused to go, but I kept going because it was helpful.

I have one brother in Holland. He has status there. The rest are in Sudan. I have been helping my twin sister a bit. She finished Khartoum University in March after doing a master's degree and a PhD. Now she's working as a teacher. Another brother was in detention for 14 months because of me. I sent some money, and with the rest of the family we paid a big amount of money to get him released. My wife was really angry about the money I sent. I didn't expect that from her. It was a big shock. That was the reason she asked me to leave the house. She wanted to be in peace so she could do her studies. In one way I do understand, so I went. I rented a room in a bungalow owned by a guy from Pakistan. I couldn't pay him straight away, until I had earned enough.

For me it wasn't about the money. It was about saving my brother's life. He was detained because of me, and that feeling would be with me the rest of my life if I didn't pay, just like my dad passed away because of me. He was in detention from 2001 until 2007, and never came out. He had been detained before, but it was in and out, in and out. People knew about my dad. A journalist wrote about him. That should be enough for my case. Let's say that they give me status: that can't take away the feeling that my dad passed away. It will be there for the rest of my life. I blame myself a lot. That's why I keep busy. The hardest thing is just before you get to sleep, when the story comes back to you.

I went to Liverpool to hand in my fresh claim in January 2015. Since then I have not heard anything. My solicitor doesn't know the full truth of my story. You need to stick with what you said to the Home Office. Once I had come into the country, by the time I knew the reality of what you should and shouldn't say or do, it was too late to fix that mistake. You can't go and tell them, 'I lied about this and that.' They will kick you out.

Gina helped me a lot at this time. When my dad passed away she and Sally*[195] were there for me. They used to take me for walks. I will never forget this. My wife didn't understand it. She got jealous – but she had lots of friends, and I wasn't allowed in to that circle. I don't hate her, but she didn't believe it. Even so, I did help her with the debt after the divorce.

In the restaurant where I worked there were a lot of Syrians. The owner rented out the house next door to some of the staff, and after I finished work I started to go there with them to eat, play cards, smoke shisha and watch movies. They would Skype their families back home in Syria and Turkey. One of the guys there had been living in Turkey with his family. He talked to me about a lot of things, and was worried about his family in Turkey. He was saying that there was no future for them in Turkey, and the war was never going to be finished in Syria, so they were planning to leave. He just needed some advice.

After that I spoke to his wife. She said she had a friend in Manchester, a Syrian doctor, and when she said the name, I knew her – she was a customer in the restaurant.

They had been to primary school together. This doctor was working for Syria Relief, and they used to come to the restaurant for meetings at the end of the day. They had a special area where they could meet. They were suspicious of other Syrians working there: maybe they thought they could be spies. I wasn't Syrian, I was Sudanese, so they trusted me. I arranged the meal for them.

When I was talking to the lady in Turkey, she asked me about my family, and I told her I had just got divorced. I told her that I didn't want a relationship with anyone right then, but that I felt I did want to get married again. I am a family type: I wasn't going to go with just any girl, sleeping around. She said she knew a friend, a Syrian who was working with her in Jordan – would it be alright to pass her my number? I thought she was joking. I never thought she would contact me. She got in touch with the lady, who was called Sara*, and then got back to me. She gave me the number, because in Arabic culture the man always has to start the relationship.

To be honest, it was uncomfortable to talk to someone you haven't seen before, but you know the reason, especially when it's a bit like an arranged marriage. In Syria it's really difficult for a woman to get married after about 25, because men are always looking for a younger woman. All Sara's sisters had married, but when she finished her degree all the problems started in Syria, and she left to work with Syria Relief. She is the organiser for a refugee centre in Jordan. We started talking by phone from time to time, just as friends at first. We were both a bit shy until we got to know each other. Then we started on Skype. I talked to her brother and sister, and asked her brother for her hand. It was hard to talk to the father – he was still in Syria.

My sister, who is teaching in Tabuk University in Saudi Arabia, went to Jordan to meet Sara and her family. It's nearly on the Jordanian border, so it's not far. They started to make arrangements for the marriage. I found out you could do it by proxy. I went to the solicitor and made an affidavit. I thought that would be it, but we found out it's really difficult. You needed affidavits, medical reports, ID, the divorce certificate, all sorts of things for the Foreign and Commonwealth Office and for the Jordanian embassy. Then I had to send everything by DHL to Jordan, either that or her dad had to be there – but he couldn't come, and in the same week that I sent the documents, he passed away. The Jordanian authorities didn't want to hold up the wedding, so they let her brother and mother just carry on. She went to the court with her mother, sister and the guy who was proxy for me, and the marriage happened!

My wife could go to study in Germany: she has got on a course there. She has also got a chance to work in Spain with a Syrian organisation. She can easily come to Europe, but she has a lot of work in Jordan, and her mum is there. When she had the wedding papers, she went to the British embassy. They told her they could do nothing if I didn't get status in the UK. Sara went to the US embassy to see if they would accept her in the American programme. At the interview they found out that her husband was in the UK, and they were surprised that I had been here for 11 years without status. They thought that something must be wrong, and said they would contact the UK to find out why I didn't have status. If they could sort that out then she could go to the US and I could come under 'family reunion' – but it could take a long time. We don't how it works really, and we are still waiting.

I still have a lot of debts. I owe friends money, and the bank takes £70 a month that I am paying back. I also took out a phone contract for a friend, and he disappeared, so I have to pay £41 for that every month. I have finished my electrical training and got Level 3, so I have good skills, but I still can't work legally. I am still doing jobs for not much money. Recently I worked in a shop, 12 hours a day for about £25. You know what the owner said to me? He said, 'You know, some people would pay to work for me.' The worst thing is, he wasn't joking! I don't know what he was thinking about himself; maybe he thought he was a god. He still owes me money.

When you work in the black economy, it's a different world – a world you don't see when you are walking around.

What about the future? I don't know, honestly. I have been away from my country for 20 years. That's longer than I lived there. In a few years I am going to be 40, and then it's downhill. I want to have kids, to have a big family. A friend of mine told me, 'You are at the best age of your life. Don't kill yourself with stress.' But how do you do that? You can't get your life back.

---

[172] The Beja people are an ethnic group of more than two million inhabiting Sudan, parts of Eritrea, Egypt and the Sahara desert. They speak the Beja language. They are made up of a number of different

tribes and are the largest ethnic group in the area of eastern Sudan between Port Sudan and Kassala.

[173] Kassala is the capital city of Kassala province in eastern Sudan. It has a population of around 500,000, and most of its inhabitants are from the Hadendoa branch of the Beja. It is an impoverished region, with infant mortality at twice the rate of Darfur.

[174] Egypt is Sudan's closest ally in North Africa. They have a long-standing historical relationship, and are connected by various cultural ties and political aspirations.

[175] It's about 570 km by road from Port Sudan to Kassala City.

[176] Omar Hassan Ahmad al-Bashir … is the president of Sudan. He came to power in 1989 when … he led … a military coup that ousted the democratically elected government of Prime Minister Sadiq al-Mahdi … In March 2009, al-Bashir became the first sitting president to be indicted by the International Criminal Court (ICC), for allegedly directing a campaign of mass killing, rape, and pillage against civilians in Darfur, [where an estimated 200-400,000 people were killed].' (https://en.wikipedia.org/wiki/Omar_al-Bashir (accessed 24th March 2016))

Kidnap, trafficking, rape and pillage are still widely used by government forces and militias to turn tribes against each other and enforce the policy of 'Arabisation' of Sudan in other areas, but it is less well documented than in Darfur.

[177] Immigration and Naturalisation Service.

[178] The CBR (Centraal Bureau Rijvaardigheid) is the Dutch Driving Test organisation. The minimum legal age to drive a moped is 16, and 18 for all other motor vehicles. In order to take the test and get a driving licence the applicant must be resident in the Netherlands, and foreigners must have a valid resident permit.

[179] On 15 January 2003 Eurodac, the EU-wide database of asylum seekers 'and irregular migrants' fingerprints, came into use. It was part of the Dublin regulations and meant that anyone who claimed asylum could be checked against the database, and if it was found that they had been fingerprinted in another EU state, they could be returned there.

[180] The initial or substantive interview.

[181] I have seen several Home Office documents with the wrong date on, or even the wrong year. Yet if an asylum seeker gets a date wrong, it

can be enough to make them 'not credible' and seriously undermine their case.

[182] National Asylum Support Service.

[183] 'The Beja Congress is a political group comprising several ethnic entities, most prominently the Beja, of the eastern region of Sudan. It was founded in 1957' (https://en.wikipedia.org/wiki/Beja_Congress (accessed 24th March 2016). At various times since then it has been banned. It has both a political and an armed wing.

[184] Once you are enrolled on a course you are allowed to continue until the end of term even if you have lost your right to public funds, but at that point you have to stop, and you cannot join another course.

[185] A weekly food parcel of basic goods worth around £8 plus bus fares from the Destitution Project at St Bride's Church in partnership with the Red Cross and Boaz Trust.

[186] When you are working illegally, it is entirely up to the employer how much he will pay – if he pays at all. There are no contracts, no set hours of employment or agreed working conditions. £2.50 an hour can hardly be called 'fair' pay, but the point Rep was making was that at least he got paid what he was promised, unlike many of the other illegal jobs he did, where the promised renumeration rarely materialised.

[187] Dallas Court Reporting Centre in Salford. See footnote 137.

[188] There are two main Immigration Removal Centres near Heathrow Airport, adjacent to each other. Rep was actually held in Harmondsworth IRC, which has a capacity of 615, making it the largest detention centre in Europe. It holds only men, and the security in several of the wings is comparable to a Category B (high-security) prison. Harmondsworth is run by a private security company called GEO.

The other, Colnbrook IRC, has a capacity of 408, and like Harmondsworth is a centre for men. People in Colnbrook are locked in their rooms at night, and during the day for roll calls. There is no freedom of movement around the centre: people are locked on the wing unless they have booked to use the facilities, in which case they are escorted by officers. Colnbrook is operated by a multinational company called Serco.

[189] Jimmy Mubenga, a healthy 46-year-old Angolan man, died on 12th October 2010 while being restrained by three G4S security guards on a

flight from Heathrow Airport to Angola. According to newspaper reports, eyewitnesses on board the flight reported that the guards used excessive force when restraining Mr Mubenga, despite the fact that he showed no signs of violence or aggression. Mr Mubenga was heard complaining that he could not breathe and that 'they are going to kill me.' Mr Mubenga left behind a widow and five children aged 1 to 17 years.

Source: 'Inquest: Briefing on the death of Jimmy Mubenga' (http://www.inquest.org.uk/pdf/briefings/INQUEST_parliamentary_in quiry_call_Jimmy_Mubenga_briefing.pdf (accessed 24th March 2016)).

[190] The bail system in the UK is haphazard at best, and downright unfair at worst. It would take a book to list the anomalies and failings. BID (Bail for Immigration Detainees) is a charity that has worked in this field for many years, and has brought out numerous reports highlighting the systemic failings (http://www.biduk.org (accessed 24th March 2016)).

[191] More than anything else, it is the 'not knowing' element of detention that drives people to despair and sometimes to attempt suicide. No one knows how long they will be there until they are given a departure date or released, and often, as in Rep's case, that is unannounced and arbitrary. Presumably there had been some hitch with the Sudanese embassy, and eventually the Home Office gave up and released him.

[192] Rep's solicitor.

[193] Because he was always working long hours, Rep has always been very slim. Nevertheless, he lost over a stone in weight while he was in detention – despite having three meals a day. He looked haggard, and his clothes were falling off. For more information on the effects of indefinite detention on asylum seekers, go to the Medical Justice website (http://www.medicaljustice.org.uk (accessed 24th March 2016)).

[194] One of his friends from the British Council.

[195] One of the Boaz Trust volunteers who had befriended and supported him.

The current refugee crisis

On 2nd September 2015 the world was shocked to see the pictures of Aylan Kurdi, a three-year-old Syrian child, washed up on a beach in Turkey. It proved to be the catalyst for a wave of compassion towards the thousands of migrants fleeing Syria and other countries in the Middle East and Africa. The British public began to offer their spare rooms for Syrians, particularly children, whether unaccompanied or in a family. As public interest mounted, so did media interest. All at once the Boaz Trust and its partners in the NACCOM network were inundated with requests from journalists and reporters.

Did we have a Syrian family that they could talk to? Could they speak to someone who was hosting a Syrian? Would it be possible to do a fly-on-the-wall documentary in the host's home? Over a period of a month there were twice as many requests for interviews than we had had in the previous 11 years.

What struck me most of all, apart from the heart-warming offers of help from across the country, was that very few people, whether journalists or Joe Public, actually had a handle on what was going on in the so-called *refugee crisis*. There were more misconceptions than there were points of understanding. For example, people seemed to think that there were Syrians arriving in the UK at that very moment, despite the fact that David Cameron had declared that the UK would not be taking *any* Syrians that came through Europe. We would definitely *not* be taking part in any quota_scheme for EU countries, whatever the quota happened to be. We had decided to opt out and leave the rest of the EU to sort out the hundreds of thousands of refugees and migrants heading north through Turkey and Greece.

Some of the offers of a spare room, kind and generous as they undoubtedly were, also demonstrated just how little people had understood the reality of the situation. It is true that the huge petition urging the government to take more Syrian refugees, which hit the 100,000 mark one day after Aylan Kurdi's death, *did* lead to a government U-turn and agreement to take 20,000 Syrians over the next five years. Originally the phrase 'up to' 20,000 was used, but then dropped when people began to question whether that meant it could still be zero. However, most people failed to realise that *all* of those 20,000 were going to be taken directly from refugee camps in Lebanon, Turkey or Jordan, and *none* of them were going to be billeted with host families. Local authorities were being asked to find surplus buildings and landlords willing to take them in.

When it was explained to potential hosts that there would be no Syrians for them to take in, but that there were plenty of asylum seekers here in the UK who were destitute and in need of a place to stay, many very generously offered to host them instead. Yet even then, it isn't so easy just to find and place a guest with many of them, because many of the offers of help just weren't feasible. The main reasons for this were that:

1. The offer is not in an area where asylum seekers are found. Locations included the fabulous offer of a room on a therapeutic farm in Kinross, Scotland, some holiday flats in Penzance, Cornwall and a caravan in Scarborough.

2. The offer was time limited. Some offered a place to stay 'for a week or ten days'. Then they would need to be moved on; the logistics would be impossible to manage.

3. The conditions of the offer, even if there was no language barrier to overcome, would make any form of supervision and contact well-nigh impossible. Two examples of this that stood out for me were a house-boat on a canal near Keighley in West Yorkshire, 'as long as they keep the engine running in winter and clean out the bilges', and a boat on the River Lea in London, 'as long as they don't mind moving every couple of weeks'.

I am not criticising any of these offers: they have been generous and heartfelt – but it does illustrate how little the general public know about asylum in the UK. Why would they, when our government seemingly has so little appetite for welcoming the stranger, and our media, for the most part, peddles inaccuracies and downright lies about vulnerable people whom they know very well can't fight back?

The government itself is not averse to pulling the wool over the eyes of its citizens. On 16th September 2015, in a statement in the House of Commons, Home Secretary Theresa May said, 'Since 2011, we have taken more than 5,000 Syrian refugees and asylum seekers.' The clear implication was that *the government* had brought them to the UK. The reality, however, was that by the end of September 2015 a mere 252 Syrians had been resettled in the UK under the Syrian Vunerable Persons Resettlement Scheme,[196] which had been launched 21 months earlier in January 2014. All the remainder of those 5,000 had *made their own way* to the UK, many brought by agents on false passports – despite the government's best (or worst) efforts to prevent that from happening.

There are, as far as I can see, only two possible explanations for what the Home Secretary said. Either she did not know the truth, which would demonstrate extraordinary ignorance for someone in charge of the asylum system, or – which is far worse – she was deliberately deceiving the Members of Parliament, and by extension the whole electorate, by taking credit for something she had not done, and indeed, had tried to prevent.

In this section I have put together a **few basic questions and answers about the crisis,** in order to give some more accurate information:

Q: So, first of all, where are all these people coming from?

A: We all know about **Syria**, where there is a war going on. Well over four million Syrians have already fled what used to be a fairly prosperous and stable country.

Then there are Eritreans, Afghans, Iraqis, Kosovars, Serbs, Pakistanis, Somalis, Nigerians and a range of other nationalities from across Africa and Asia. In the first nine months of 2015 the main countries of origin of asylum seekers, accounting for almost half of the total, were Syria (20%), Afghanistan (7%), Kosovo (6%), Eritrea (6%) and Serbia (5%).

Q: Are they economic migrants?

(I object to the term 'economic migrant', not because it doesn't describe a category of people accurately, but because it's only ever used for people coming *into* the Western world, and never for those going *out*. If you go to work in Germany or Australia, guess what? *You* are an economic migrant! Maybe we need to start calling economic migrants who come *here* 'expats', since expat is just a shortened version of 'expatriate', and actually means 'a person temporarily or permanently residing, as an immigrant, in a country other than that of their citizenship.'[197] That would throw the tabloids into a frenzy! However, for the purposes of this book, I'll stick with *economic migrant*.)

A: The devastating civil war in **Syria** is forcing millions to leave their homes, and is the largest humanitarian crisis of our time. Very few from Syria can be classed as economic migrants, as a quick internet search will quickly demonstrate, but what about the others?

Kosovo and Serbia are both European countries, and it seems that the majority of those fleeing *have* done so for economic reasons: simply put, they have no jobs. Young people, in particular, have taken the opportunity to join the exodus. Very few – probably less than one per cent, will be granted refugee status, and most are being repatriated as quickly as possible.

Eritrea is a small country in North East Africa. It is a communist dictatorship. There is compulsory military service, which may last to age 40. Evangelical Christians, Jehovah's Witnesses and especially Pentecostals are subject to brutal persecution. Church leaders are imprisoned and tortured. Evangelism is forbidden, and even small house meetings are raided and the believers arrested. Prison is often underground with no natural light, or a container in the desert with 20 people in – it's 40 degrees during the day, and minus ten at night. *Open Doors* ranks Eritrea as third in its World Watch List of countries where Christians are most persecuted.[198]

Afghanistan is a very dangerous place. Although the Home Office deports Afghans in charter planes, the Foreign and Commonwealth Office advises that it's not safe. The UN documented 3,545 civilian deaths in 2015. The total of more than 11,000 casualties was the highest since the UN began keeping systematic records in 2009. Many of those young Afghans in the 'Jungle' in Calais have lost parents or siblings to Taliban atrocities. In addition, there are many who were interpreters for the allied forces. The UK has given refuge only to some, and refused most. Ninety-four per cent of the estimated 3,000 interpreters have reported death threats.

Iraq is equally dangerous. Many of us will be familiar with what Daesh or IS, or whatever you want to call it, did to the Yazidis.[199] They have done exactly the same to Christians, most of whom have fled the country.[200] A recent

UNAMI (UN Assistance Mission for Iraq) report highlighted kidnappings, enslavement and sexual violence. It also gave specifics about executions by shooting, beheading, bulldozing, burning alive and throwing people off the top of buildings:

> Since January 2014 we have seen more than 18,000 people killed as a result of the conflict. In addition more than three million people fled their houses, communities and became internally displaced people.

An estimated 3,500 people are 'currently being held in slavery by ISIL,' according to the report.[201]

The bottom line is that the vast majority of the million plus people who fled north through Europe in 2015 were genuine refugees.

Q: What is Europe doing about the crisis?

A: As I write this, the situation in Europe is a mess. Germany and Sweden initially led the way in welcoming the refugees. Germany in particular extended an open hand, officially taking an unprecedented 476,000 asylum applications in 2015, but recently there has been a backlash, particularly from right-wing groups. Dealing with hundreds of thousands of new arrivals has understandably been very difficult.

There is a quota system for taking refugees direct from Greece and Italy, both of which bear the brunt of the crisis, but only five European countries have agreed to take more than 5,000. At the same time, several countries have now closed their borders to refugees, leaving tens of thousands stranded in makeshift camps, waiting for someone to open the gate so they can continue their journey. The UK, of course, has opted out of the quota system.

Q: What sort of numbers are we talking about?

A: By the time this book is published they will be out of date, but here are a few statistics that offer a comparison:

1. **1.3 million** refugees came to Europe in 2015. That has added all of **0.0175 per cent** to its 740 million inhabitants.

2. There are more than **4 million** displaced Syrians in Turkey, Lebanon and Jordan alone. **1.4 million** of them are in Lebanon, which is the size of Yorkshire, and mainly mountainous.

3. **One-third** of the population of Lebanon is made up of Syrian and Palestinian refugees.

4. The United Kingdom has pledged to take **20,000** Syrians direct from camps in the Middle East over five years. That leaves **99.5 per cent of them** still there (plus, of course, the new arrivals).

5. Just before the bulldozers came to demolish the 'Jungle' at Calais, volunteers took a census. They found that there were 5,497 residents in total. That represents just 0.4% of all those seeking refuge in Europe. 423 were unaccompanied children.

OK, so what can we *do* about it?

For the answer to this question, you need one piece of equipment – a mirror. *Whoever* you are, and *wherever* you are – **you** are the answer!

No, I'm not going to just leave it at that – I *will* offer some practical suggestions. They are not prescriptive. If you have imagination, I'm sure you can figure out lots more.

They are not specifically aimed at churches, but I do believe that churches are ideally placed to deliver on them, just as they are already doing in other areas where the state is shrinking and services are being cut. As a follower of Jesus, I am convinced that His Church, which is His body (and therefore His feet, arms, hands and voice – everything except the head!) is the ultimate answer to all of society's ills. We have made a difference to street and gun crime through *Street Pastors,* to clubbers through *Street Angels,* to youth disaffection through many church youth clubs and projects like The Message Trust, to poverty and debt through food banks and CAP centres… the list is endless, and growing.

So why not refugees and asylum seekers too?

Ten ways you can get involved

You may live 100 miles from the nearest refugee, but there are still things in this list that you can do – and if you live in an asylum dispersal area, a whole lot more!

1. **Get informed**. It's fairly simple, but if you don't know what's going on, you can't know what to do about it.

Keep up with the news: I personally find Al-Jazeera has the best TV analysis of refugee issues, and *The Guardian* or *The Independent* probably the best newspaper coverage. Subscribe to good refugee NGO mailings. Apart from the Boaz Trust and NACCOM (I *am* biased), there is lots of good information from the Refugee Council, Refugee Action, Detention Action, City of Sanctuary and a host of other websites.

2. Once you are informed, you can **pray effectively.** Prayer is not an excuse for doing nothing. In fact, if you pray, you may well find that your prayers are answered by God empowering *you* to be part of the solution to your prayers.

3. **Be a welcomer.** As you have already seen from the refugee stories, things go wrong in the asylum system when there is no one there to help and support at the start of the process. Find out if there is a refugee drop-in in your town or city. Is there a welcome scheme in existence? If not, could you or your church/community start one? Have a look at the *Welcome Boxes* website, (http://www.cinnamonnetwork.co.uk/refugees).

4. **Be a friend.** As one young lady, who had been taken in by a couple, once said, 'Even more important than having a roof over my head was having a friend.' If you have asylum seekers in your church, take time out to befriend them. It doesn't have to be heavy, and shouldn't be one-way either. It's about making time to chat, to be there for them and, if necessary, to go that bit further. If there aren't any asylum seekers in your

church then see if you can find some. Your local City of Sanctuary group is a great place to start (www.cityofsanctuary.org).

5. **Use your skills.** If you have skills, can you share them? People need jobs when they get their status – can you help train them up? Maybe you have a trade – can they learn from you, shadow you, borrow your tools? Are you a teacher, or maybe retired? Many refugees need to learn English, either formally through ESOL classes or informally in a conversation club or just meeting for a chat. Could you teach people to knit, or sew, or paint... why not share your expertise? Are you a medic? What better way to spend your vacation than on a beach... treating the sick as they come off rickety boats in Lesvos or Lampedusa!

6. **Offer your spare room.** There are a growing number of *hosting schemes* in the UK, and people are offering their spare rooms for destitute asylum seekers or refugees. It's not illegal, and it is a fantastic blessing to really vulnerable people. Have a look on the NACCOM website (www.naccom.org.uk) for your nearest project, or post a query on the contact page. If you are interested in fostering or adopting an unaccompanied minor from Syria, then that can be done through *Home for Good* (www.homeforgood.org.uk).

7. **Help people transition to refugee status.** I guess this can only be done if you are attached to an organisation where asylum seekers are already coming to drop-ins or accessing other services, but it's a really vital

service. You might even consider setting one up yourself. It would involve helping people access accommodation and benefits, understand and manage utilities, move into new accommodation and generally integrate. You don't have to be an expert to do most of this. Just accompanying someone to the Job Centre can be a huge help.

8. **Visit people in detention.** As you have read in these stories, nothing is as degrading and depressing as being detained without cause. Having a friend who will visit, listen and pray may well save someone's life. AVID has a list of visitors' groups on its website (www.aviddetention.org.uk).

9. **Campaign.** Asylum seekers have no voice of their own, so they need *our* voices. There are regular campaign actions on the Refugee Action website, as well as Still Human Still Here and Detention Action. There is also a toolkit for refused asylum seekers to start their own personal campaign on the Right to Remain website. Or maybe you could start your own campaign through Avaaz, Change.org, or 38 Degrees.

10. **Give.** This does not necessarily involve money... but it sure helps when there isn't much available! It is especially helpful for small grassroots organisations trying to grow, and particularly those who are offering accommodation to people who have no recourse to public funds – i.e. refused asylum seekers – because there is no statutory funding for them.

But it could also mean giving of your time, your skills, your surplus... some people just happen to have an empty house knocking around which could be put to good use accommodating some very vulnerable people!

If you can't find anything to do from those ten ideas, please get in touch. Like I said, it's not an exhaustive list!

I will finish with two quotes from William Wilberforce, who did much to end the slave trade in his generation, yet never lived to see its abolition. Wilberforce is one of my heroes, primarily because he never gave up on the task God had given him. For him, getting the truth out to the world was the first step to abolition. He worked tirelessly for many years to inform people of the reality of slavery. Then he could say, 'You may choose to look the other way but you can never say again that you did not know'.[202]

I pray that will be true of every man and woman in this country, starting with me and you. There were many challenges and many disappointments on the way, but that did not stop him or his faith in God. In 1830, not long before his death, Wilberforce wrote this in a letter explaining that his physician had advised him not to attend an abolitionist meeting:

Our motto must continue to be perseverance. And ultimately I trust the Almighty will crown our efforts with success.[203]

And success did come. Let's persevere, pray and work until the UK asylum system is transformed, just and compassionate, and the destitution, detention and degradation of refugees in our country and beyond is abolished, just as slavery was in Wilberforce's day.[204]

[196] 'Home Office quarterly statistics', Q3 July–September 2015, 26th November 2015
(https://www.gov.uk/government/statistics/immigration-statistics-july-to-september-2015 (accessed 24th March 2016)).

[197] https://en.wikipedia.org/wiki/Expatriate (accessed 24th March 2016).

[198] http://www.opendoorsuk.org/persecution/worldwatch/eritrea.php (accessed 24th March 2016).

[199] The Yazidis are a Kurdish religious community with their own distinct culture and monotheistic beliefs. By far the largest community, around 650,000, live in Iraq. There are smaller communities in Armenia, Georgia, Turkey, Iran, Syria and Germany.

In August 2014 ISIL overran Sinjar in Iraq. 200,000 people fled, including 40,000 Yazidis. Because ISIL regards Yazidis as devil-worshippers, those who could not escape were executed, and thousands of young girls were abducted as sex slaves.

[200] Before the invasion of Iraq there were 1.2 million Christians in the country. Because Christians are associated with the West, Iraqi Christians bore the brunt of revenge attacks after Saddam Hussein was ousted from power. There are now only 250,000 Christians left in Iraq, and numbers are decreasing daily with the ongoing danger of churches being bombed, Christians murdered and the threat of IS taking more territory. Open Doors rates Iraq as the second most dangerous place in the world for Christians.
(http://www.opendoorsuk.org/persecution/worldwatch/iraq.php (accessed 24th March 2016))

[201] A summary of the report can be found at
http://www.newsjs.com/url.php?p=http://www.ibtimes.co.in/un-iraq-conflict-report-18000-killed-3-million-displaced-under-two-years-isis-holds-3500-sex-663796 (accessed 24th March 2016).

[202] Wilberforce said this at the close of a speech in the House of Commons in 1791.

[203] http://www.azquotes.com/quote/553072 (accessed 24th March 2016).

[204] Although the Slavery Abolition Act of 1833 abolished slavery throughout the British Empire, in recent years it has re-emerged in new, modern forms, even here in the UK. Christian agencies are

leading the way in combatting this new and growing evil. The Evangelical Alliance has an excellent summary of anti-slavery groups at http://www.eauk.org/current-affairs/politics/modern-slavery/anti-slavery-groups.cfm (accessed 13th April 2016).

About Dave Smith

Dave Smith is the founder of two Manchester-based charities, Mustard Tree[205] (1993) and the Boaz Trust[206] (2004). The Boaz Trust now manages 14 houses, a night shelter scheme and a hosting scheme. It accommodates around 50 destitute, refused asylum seekers and 20 refugees.

In 2013 Dave was awarded the British Empire Medal for 'Services to the Community'. After attempting, without success, to engage with the new government's Big Society ideas, he returned the BEM a year later in protest at the increasingly draconian immigration legislation.

His first book, *The Book of Boaz*, was published by Instant Apostle in June 2014. It contains both a brief history of the Boaz Trust and a sharp critique of the asylum system, along with a call for justice.

Dave coordinates NACCOM,[207] the national 'No Accommodation' network, which comprises 34 member groups across the UK accommodating destitute asylum seekers. It became a CIO (Charitable Incorporated Organisation) in June 2015.

He has spoken at numerous conferences and festival events, including Greenbelt, Spring Harvest, New Wine and Catalyst. His great passion is to end asylum destitution in the UK.

Dave lives in Manchester with his wife Shona, who is a teacher of the deaf, and son Caleb. He has four older children and three grandchildren.

---

[205] http://www.mustardtree.org.uk (accessed 24th March 2016)
[206] http://www.boaztrust.org.uk (accessed 24th March 2016)
[207] http://www.naccom.org.uk (accessed 24th March 2016)

Also by Dave Smith

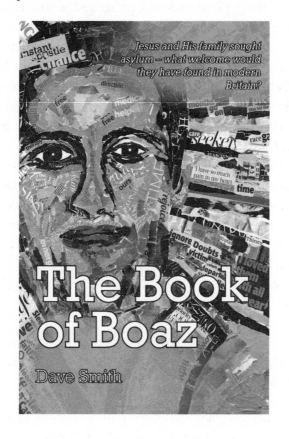

The 'failed' asylum seeker.
Confused. Bewildered. Hungry. Cold. Scared.
Or
Illegal. Criminal. Guilty. Cheating. Dangerous.
Which is it?

Dave Smith set up the Boaz Trust ten years ago to fight the cause of the asylum seeker. Confronted with a media that can seem more determined to demonise than to tell the truth, and with a political class who appear happier to scapegoat than to stand for justice, this has not been an easy battle. Yet his biggest enemy has been the seemingly cruelly inefficient and impersonal bureaucracy that needlessly condemns so many asylum seekers to near-destitution and despair.

The Book of Boaz is a story of how compassion and truth have inspired the author and others to shout for those who are too traumatised to even whisper for themselves. Dave Smith is a politically astute, articulate and straight-talking campaigner who is passionate about justice and freedom. His guide to the asylum world will leave you, like it leaves everyone who enters the system, with radically different views.

'[The work of the Boaz Trust is] beautiful and redemptive.'
Shane Claiborne, author of The Irresistible Revolution and founder of The Simple Way

'I was delighted to become a patron for the Boaz Trust, because they transform the lives of destitute asylum seekers ... who have been unable to access support and have nowhere else to turn to for help.'
John Leech, MP for Manchester Withington

Published by Instant Apostle (September 2014)
ISBN 978 1 909728 17 2
RRP £9.99